LEVEL ONE
TEACHER GUIDE

PUBLISHED BY

The CiRCE Institute is a non-profit 501(c)3 organization that exists to promote and support classical education in the school and in the home. We seek to identify the ancient principles of learning, to communicate them enthusiastically, and to apply them vigorously in today's educational settings through curricula development, teacher training, events, an online academy, and a content-laden website.

CIRCE INSTITUTE
81 McCachern Blvd, Concord, NC, 28025
704.795.7944 | info@circeinstitute.org
www.circeinstitute.org

ALL RIGHTS RESERVED.
NO PART OF THIS PROGRAM MAY BE REPRODUCED IN ANY FORM,
BY ANY MEANS, WITHOUT WRITTEN PERMISSION FROM THE PUBLISHER.
© 2015 by the CiRCE Institute. Second printing.

PERMISSIONS

Teachers who purchase or for whom schools purchase the complete *The Lost Tools of Writing*™ package are granted permission to duplicate pages from the Teacher's Guide for their personal use. They are also granted permission to copy pages from the Teacher's Guide as reference pages for their students, including, but not limited to, the assessment guides provided in this Teacher's Guide.

One Student Workbook should be purchased for each student who is taught *The Lost Tools of Writing*™. Some Invention worksheets will be imitated more than once. If the teacher or student wishes to copy these pages, they may do so, but only for the individual student who possesses the Student Workbook. Students are also encouraged to imitate the pattern of the worksheet on their own paper.

Permission is not granted to copy worksheets or exercise forms or any other material from one student's workbook for other students.

Permission is granted for quotations and short excerpts to be used in published materials with the condition that the source of those quotations and excerpts is included in the published materials.

For longer excerpts, please contact us at www.circeinstitute.org.

ACKNOWLEDGEMENTS

The Lost Tools of Writing is the product of a vast team effort.

Hundreds of teachers and students have experienced *The Lost Tools of Writing*™, and many have been generous with their suggestions and feedback. This fifth edition is our enthusiastic "Thank You!!" to everyone who helped us make *The Lost Tools of Writing*™ the best composition program in the world.

The authors of this Fifth Edition are Leah Lutz and Andrew Kern, with contributions from Camille Goldston, Renee Mathis, David Kern, and Arlene Roemer da Feltre.

Special acknowledgement is due to the members and alumni of the CiRCE Institute Apprenticeship, who have taught, practiced, reviewed, and developed *The Lost Tools of Writing*™ in their various contexts.

Furthermore, thank you to all who have participated in a *Lost Tools Of Writing*™ Workshop, to teachers who have been part of an in-house *Lost Tools Of Writing*™ Teacher Training, to parents who stole a Saturday from their busy schedules, and to heads of school who demonstrated their commitment to classical education when they supported their teachers' efforts to achieve excellence in both classical composition and classical teaching.

The CiRCE Institute is a not-for-profit corporation, dependent upon and grateful for the generosity of benefactors who share her vision for classical education. If not for the tremendous support of so many fellow believers, *The Lost Tools of Writing*™ would never have seen the light of day. You have sustained us, and it would be wrong to fail to acknowledge and thank you.

TABLE *of* CONTENTS

Preface – vii

INTRODUCTION
Part One: Foundations for Writing – 3
Part Two: Sequence and Schedules: A Proposed Plan of Action – 13
Part Three: Introducing the Lesson Guides – 23

The Introductory Lesson: The Three Writing Challenges – 31

ESSAY ONE
Invention: From Issue to ANI – 37
Arrangement: From ANI to Outline – 45
Elocution: From Outline to Essay - 53

ESSAY TWO
Invention: The Five Common Topics - 61
Arrangement: A Guide to Sorting – 69
Elocution: Parallelism I - 81

ESSAY THREE
Invention: Comparison I: Similarities - 93
Arrangement: A Guide to Exordium – 99
Elocution: Verbs - 107

ESSAY FOUR
Invention: Comparison II: Degree & Kind - 117
Arrangement: A Guide to Amplification – 125
Elocution: Parallelism II - 133

ESSAY FIVE
Invention: Definition - 143
Arrangement: A Guide to Division – 151
Elocution: Antithesis - 161

TABLE *of* CONTENTS

ESSAY SIX
Invention: Circumstance - 171
Arrangement: A Guide to Refutation – 177
Elocution: Simile – 187

ESSAY SEVEN
Invention: Relation - 197
Arrangement: A Guide to Narratio – 207
Elocution: Alliteration – 217

ESSAY EIGHT
Invention: Testimony - 229
Arrangement: Review – 239
Elocution: Metaphor – 241

ESSAY NINE
Invention: Review - 253
Arrangement: Review – 255
Elocution: Assonance - 259

APPENDICES
Appendix A: How to Edit - 267
Appendix B: A Guide to Assessment – 275
Appendix C: Essay Templates – 287
Appendix D: On Mimetic Teaching - 295
Appendix E: FAQs – 299
Appendix F: Glossary - 305
Appendix G: Resources – 313
Appendix H: Lesson Summaries - 319
Appendix I: Sample Essays - 335

PREFACE
A Note to the Teacher

---

*"Times are bad.
Children no longer obey their parents,
and everyone is writing a book."*

MARCUS TULLIUS CICERO

Welcome to a treasure chest of resources used by teachers around the world to cultivate wisdom and virtue through writing. Welcome to a toolbox used by students around the world to remove guesswork, anxiety, and frustration from the writing experience. *The Lost Tools of Writing*™ equips you to teach with purposeful clarity and your students to learn with well-earned confidence.

Good writers are both disciplined and creative, using tools effectively and able to explore ideas far beyond the formula of a five-paragraph essay. You may be writing a poem, an essay, or a story; or you may be completing an assignment for school or work and want to do it successfully. Either way, without the confidence that you can combine creativity and discipline, your writing will never satisfy you.

The Lost Tools of Writing™ equips you with tools and resources to cultivate the discipline and creativity that mark effective writers (and readers and thinkers, for that matter).

Like many writers, we searched for many years for the "secrets" of good writing. Here's what we found: there are no secrets. The "tricks" have long been available to anybody who wants them.

You and your students don't need a new piece of technology, a new technique, or some hidden formula that makes writing easy and frees you from the need to think. You need honest tools to help you master writing with all its difficulties. Besides, just when you feel you've mastered the latest technology or technique, you learn that a new one has been developed. Or, you find that you have graduated to a new level of skill and have outgrown the trick.

There is no new technique or method because the tools have been known and used since even before people wrote. How can that be? Because writing on paper, parchment, or a screen is only a record of something that has previously happened in the mind.

In the classical tradition, we've found simpler, amazingly effective resources that focus your instruction on the thinking that leads to good writing. We've discovered tools that integrate writing into the curriculum in a way that cultivates your students' ability to think, to read, to make decisions, and, yes, to write.

You have in your hands a refinement of over twenty years of discoveries about effective writing. It is a guide to cultivating both creativity and discipline. We have spent thousands of hours "digging up" these lost tools and coaching teachers and students in their use, helping them solve the three universal challenges of writing.

The tools we have discovered work for students and teachers in every learning context, at every grade level, even in college and on the job. That is because they answer the universal challenges that every writer and thinker has to handle. In the *Lost Tools of Writing Level I* we have applied these tools to the middle and upper school years. A ninth grader with very little writing background needs these tools. A middle school student with some preparation in reading and writing is ready for them. If you know a high school or college student who has not discovered them, be merciful: introduce them. Their teachers, their professors, and they themselves will thank you!

Teachers and parents want to cultivate creative discipline and disciplined creativity in themselves and their students. Many teachers are successful because they know intuitively that writing requires both creativity and discipline. But often they are not sure how to bring them together.

On the one hand, you want proven tools that can help students explore the texts they read, the experiences they live, and their own minds. On the other, you want to refine the skills and virtues that will give your students the focused attention and thoughtfulness that empower and guide the journey toward wisdom.

These tools and skills are available to schools and home schools. Children will learn how to gather information, sort it, and express it in effective and appropriate ways. They will learn how to write and how to think.

In the Teacher Guide and Student Workbook the material is presented in a logical sequence so that, through this ordered presentation, you will be able to see both the "big-picture" and the specific daily steps that you will follow with your students.

You can only feel the effectiveness and simplicity of the LTW through experience. We want you to discover not only that it is possible to teach writing, but that you already know almost everything you need to teach it effectively. You have been digging up information, sorting it, and using it to express ideas since before you went to school. The basic skills you've already developed will be refined and cultivated both in yourself and in your students. Somewhere around the third lesson, you will begin to realize that you have discovered tools with unimaginable power (although even the first has surprised and delighted many teachers and students).

Over the twenty years teaching and leading workshops on classical rhetoric, we've watched hundreds of teachers and students gain the confidence that comes from the unique combination of skill and knowledge developed by LTW. The promise of *The Lost Tools of Writing*™ was well expressed by our friend Amanda who said, "I have taught in various teaching environments from private tutoring to homeschooling to public school. None of the writing curricula I used comes close to the quality and depth of *The Lost Tools of Writing*™."

THE FEATURES OF THE LOST TOOLS OF WRITING
The Lost Tools of Writing includes the following tools to assist you as you teach your students to write:

1. Online audio and video streaming that introduce you to the purpose, structure, and tools of *The Lost Tools of Writing*.

2. This Teacher's Guide including the following elements:

- An Introduction with three detailed parts:
    - *Part One: Foundations for Writing*
    - *Part Two: Sequence & Schedules: A Proposed Plan of Action*
    - *Part Three: Introducing the Lesson Guides*

- A Year-at-a-Glance Chart that presents *the sequence and schedule by which you will teach the lessons.*

- A Lesson Sequence that *maps a potential weekly process by which you can teach each lesson.*

- Lesson Guides with *lesson plans, sample worksheets, and much more.*

- Appendices, *including all essay templates (or outlines), FAQs, a glossary, recommended resources, simplified lesson summaries, and information on assessment and the Mimetic teaching sequence.*

3. A Student Workbook complete with worksheets, exercise forms, templates, and samples essays for each lesson. The combination of the Teacher's Guide and Student Workbook provides you the necessary parts to teach this curriculum.

4. External support for you as a teacher, including:

- The *LTW Mentor,* a Yahoo Group that provides you with articles, tips, and samples.

- The CiRCE Apprenticeship, a program that offers teachers the chance to participate in intensive, on-going instruction with the CiRCE Head Mentors and other teachers from all over the country, on the theory and practice of Christian Classical Education. For details, visit our website at www.circeinstitute.org/apprenticeship.

- Workshops around the country presented by CiRCE Certified Master Teachers. To plan a *Lost Tools of Writing* workshop in your area email info@circeinstitute.org.

INTRODUCTION

PART ONE
Foundations for Writing

The Lost Tools of Writing are necessary for every writer, but they are not sufficient. To master the craft, the writer must walk "five paths," as it were, each of which develops different dimensions of the art of writing.

The first is the *literary* path, which simply means that you must read deep and wide. Every great writer is a great reader: patient, attentive, curious, and interested. We contend that no books better train writers than the Bible (especially the King James Version for its poetic and literary qualities), Homer's *Iliad* and *Odyssey*, Virgil's *Aeneid*, and Shakespeare's better plays. We internalize what we read, so it is important to read excellent writing worth imitating.

The second is the *linguistic* path, which names the need to translate from another language into your own. The translator perpetually asks two simple, but not always easy, questions: Which word or phrase should I use? and, Where should I put it? The writer continually asks the same questions, so translation of great works provides effective training. Furthermore, translating is like writing in slow motion. You are imitating what others have written and also making your own judgments about how to do it. We recommend an inflected language because it focuses attention on word placement, and because Greek and Latin, both inflected languages, contain the foundational literary and historical works that everything since the classical world has been built on.

The third is the *critical* or *technical* path. The better a writer knows the rules and conventions of grammar and usage, the more freely he can move among ideas. As early and as gently as possible, students should learn the parts of speech, the role each plays, and the rules that govern consistent, careful thinking and expression. If they have to think about them too much while they are writing, the pleasure and effectiveness of writing is inhibited. The rules are not made by grammar teachers. Rather, they are drawn from the logic of consistent thinking and the practices of the great thinkers, writers, and communicators. When you use them well, you are imitating the masters of the language.

Fourth, writers must take some steps down the *theoretical* path, which takes a lifetime to master. While walking down this path, you strive to understand writing's purpose and nature, its powers and limits (e.g. propriety, consistency), elements (e.g. words, sentences, and chapters), and forms (e.g. essays, short stories, poems). Take your time to reflect on and research these rather large ideas and don't let them overwhelm you. Any wisdom you gain will enable you to write better. Perhaps more importantly, you'll become a more effective writing teacher by applying your growing understanding.

> **THE 5 PATHS TO**
> *Quality Writing*
> 1. The Literary Path
> 2. The Linguistic Path
> 3. The Critical Path
> 4. The Theoretical Path
> 5. The Practical Path

The fifth path is the *practical* path, which is what *The Lost Tools of Writing* directly equips you for. Writing is a skill that requires coaching and practice. LTW introduces students to the essential writing tools and lays out a sequence of exercises that guides them step by step to the complete persuasive essay. When they walk the practical path, they imitate the very thought processes of the great writers.

We have said there are five paths, but there are two more experiences writers need for their writing to inspire. First, they need to live a little so they have something to write about. And second, they need what Shakespeare called "a muse of fire." When the flame of insight rests upon a person who lacks the tools and skills to express it, it will cool. Both muse and writer leave frustrated. On the other hand, if they master all the tools but inspiration never comes, the writing won't sing the heart of their ideas, only the outer surface. Ah, but if the muse of fire descends . . .

Walk the five paths, live a little, and pray for inspiration, and your writing and that of your students will sing. But don't feel overwhelmed. If you take one step down any path, your writing will be better for it. Give your students time in their youth for all the paths. For yourself, take any steps you can with a grateful heart. Nobody has ever walked any path to its limits. All of us have walked them at least a little way. A very few have gone a long way down them all. Those are the ones the aspiring writer will follow.

THE CANONS OF COMPOSITION

Classical rhetoric consists of five Canons that order the rhetorician's task. The first three define the writing process. *The Lost Tools of Writing*™ is built upon the understanding that these three Canons provide solutions to the three universal writing challenges. This section begins by discussing those three challenges and concludes by describing their solutions.

THE THREE PROBLEMS EVERY WRITER FACES

If we were to ask you what you find challenging when you write, what would you say? When we ask this question during *The Lost Tools of Writing*™ workshops we hear answers like these:

- Getting started
- Finding facts
- Spelling
- Grammar
- Defending my argument
- Moving the reader
- Arranging my ideas
- Transitioning from one thought to the next
- Being convincing
- Having enough to say
- Not saying too much
- Saying it just right

Sound familiar? Do you notice that they all fit into one of three broad categories:

1. Coming up with ideas — *invention*
2. Putting your ideas in order – *arrangement*
3. Expressing your ideas appropriately – *elocution*

These are the universal writing challenges every writer faces. If you can solve them, you can write effectively. Put simply, to write well is to come up with something to say, to put your materials in the best order, and to express your thoughts appropriately.

THE THREE SOLUTIONS

Solving these three challenges was the goal of classical rhetoricians like Aristotle, Cicero, and Quintilian. They noticed that people overcome them by working through three stages, one for each challenge. They gave these stages names, translated into English as follows:

- **Invention** (coming up with ideas—sometimes called Discovery)
- **Arrangement** (ordering your ideas—sometimes called Disposition)
- **Elocution** (expressing your ideas appropriately—sometimes called Style)

These solutions comprise the three Canons of classical composition (Canon means "a standard of measure" or a "body of rules") Later, when your students practice the complete program of classical rhetoric, including speech, they will add the Canons of Memory and Delivery.

In each lesson or essay, your student will practice Invention, Arrangement, and Elocution separately and in that order, acquiring tools for each canon, then putting them together in a new essay.

In short, writing students learn to discover material, to arrange this material, and to communicate it appropriately. Simple. But not always easy! Each takes practice, which must be guided and coached.

GUIDE TO INVENTION: THE FIVE COMMON TOPICS

> *"A modern textbook of rhetoric deals largely with style — choice of words, figures of speech, formation of sentences, arrangement of paragraphs. An ancient Rhetoric . . . is concerned with matter as well as with style. Invention, or the discovery of ideas and subject matter, was the first and perhaps the most important section of any formal treatise on rhetoric."*
>
> ~ ***Cicero***

As Cicero indicated so long ago, the first key to writing is not clarity or vigor or mechanics. The first and most important — and perhaps most overlooked — challenge remains what Cicero called "the discovery of ideas" or coming up with something to say.

The Lost Tools of Writing™, therefore, begins by imitating *the thought process* the writer pursues to discover subject matter. The first of the three Canons is Invention.

ASKING QUESTIONS

In a word, the writer begins by asking questions. Indeed, we are always asking questions, because it is in our nature to do so. That makes Invention natural, if not always easy. The Canon of Invention identifies and practices the common questions your students have been asking since they were very young children.

Students learn that the beginning of every paper is the big question they ask. Then they practice using the tools, one at a time, to answer their questions.

QUESTIONS AS TOOLS

Ironically, perhaps, those tools are more questions. The essay guides in Chapter Four explain how to introduce and coach these question-tools in LTW I. Five exceptionally powerful questions are presented to your students, which they will use to gather ideas, information, and insight for their essays. They are called "Topics" because they are "places" you visit to gather information ("topic" comes from a Greek word for place).

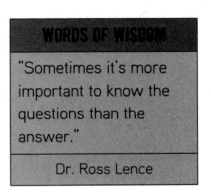

WORDS OF WISDOM

"Sometimes it's more important to know the questions than the answer."

Dr. Ross Lence

These Five Common Topics of Invention you will teach this year are:

> *Comparison:* How does X compare with/to Y?
> *Definition:* Who or What is X? What kind of thing is X?
> *Circumstance:* What are the circumstances surrounding X?
> *Relation:* How is X related to Y?
> *Testimony:* Who says what about X?

By adding one topic to each new essay, your students learn to discover an abundance of information, thus solving the first writing challenge.

You will teach the topics according to the following pattern:

Invention Lesson One teaches the ANI Chart.

Lesson two introduces the topics of Invention, which are then developed in the following lessons as follows:

Comparison (Lessons Three and Four)
How is X similar to Y?
How is X different from Y?

Definition (Lesson Five)
What is X?
Who is X?
What kind of thing is X?

Circumstance (Lesson Six)

What was happening in the same place and time as your issue or situation?

What was happening at the same time, but in different places from your issue or situation?

Relation (Lesson Seven)

What led to the situation in which a decision needs to be made?

What followed the decision?

Testimony (Lesson Eight)

What do witnesses say about the issue?

Once your students have employed these topics to discover and generate ideas, they will, like a miner rising from a mine, need to sort the dross from the gold. Then they can organize their materials for their essays.

That brings us to the second Canon: Arrangement.

GUIDE TO ARRANGEMENT: ELEMENTS & TEMPLATES

Arrangement is the art by which a writer selects, sorts, and outlines ideas and subject matter.

The arrangement of an essay is like the design of a house. Having generated ideas, the architect creates the blueprints. To do so, he applies the invariable principles of structure so the house can fulfill its purpose as a safe, sturdy dwelling.

So it is with the framing of a written text. The outline of a persuasive essay is derived from and suited to the nature of a persuasive essay. The structure of a novel is derived from and suited to the nature of a novel. The structure has to fit the nature and purpose of the text.

Therefore, the Canon of Arrangement teaches students to order their thoughts according to the nature and purpose of a persuasive essay.

By learning the outline one element at a time, your students learn to construct rather elaborate essays. Though they begin with a very simple and even tedious three-paragraph essay, by the end of the year, they write complete (eleven paragraphs or more) persuasive essays.

The Arrangement materials for each essay include an Exercise Page, a Student Worksheet, and a Template. The Exercise Pages are used to apply the lesson's new idea, the Worksheets show students how to order their subject matter in the right pattern, and the Template provides a model outline that includes the new essay element. Each Arrangement Lesson through Essay Seven adds one element to the Persuasive Essay.

Arrangement One orders the Rudimentary Persuasive Essay (RPE), a simple, tedious outline with only the most fundamental parts of the persuasive essay.

Through the Arrangement lesson in Essay Two, your students learn the powerful tool of sorting, which teaches them to order and select appropriate information from their ever-growing Invention. They create an outline for a conventional five-paragraph Introductory Persuasive Essay (IPE) with a simple introduction and conclusion.

Essays Three and Four Arrangement provide tools for introductions and conclusions: the Exordium and Amplification, enabling them to outline a Basic Persuasive Essay (BPE).

Arrangement for Essays Five and Six shows students how to respond to opposition to their argument, adding a Division and a Refutation ("divisio" and "refutatio" in Latin), thus expanding the BPE.

Finally, in Arrangement for Essay Seven, students add a statement of facts, or "Narratio," and they write their first Complete Persuasive Essay (CPE).

Arrangement Eight and Nine review the Complete Persuasive Essay, adding new lessons to Invention and Elocution.

Through the Arrangement lessons, your students acquire tools to solve the first two writing challenges: they have something to say and they have ordered their subject matter. Only one challenge remains: to express their ideas appropriately.

GUIDE TO ELOCUTION: BASIC EDITING, SCHEMES, & TROPES

"Like stones, words are laborious and unforgiving, and the fitting of them together, like the fitting of stones, demands great patience and strength of purpose and particular skill."

Edmund Morrison

Elocution is the art of expressing one's ideas appropriately.

By practicing the Canon of Elocution, your students learn to turn their outlines into sentences and paragraphs and to revise their essays with basic editing, schemes, and tropes.

For the first essay, Elocution is so easy it is tedious. Students merely convert the outline into sentences and paragraphs. However, by the end of the year, your students acquire the tools to "suit the action to the words, the words to the action," as Shakespeare's Hamlet said.

Basic Editing	**Schemes**	**Tropes**
1. Precise and Active Verbs	1. Parallelism	1. Simile
	2. Antithesis	2. Metaphor
	3. Alliteration	
	4. Assonance	

Your students will need time to learn to use these schemes and tropes appropriately. First they just need to learn them and even use them badly. Gradually, they will develop a sense for when and how to use them, but do not demand mature judgment from students who are only learning to handle the tools.

SUMMARY

You have now been introduced to the basic concepts of Invention, Arrangement, and Elocution, the solutions to the three universal writing challenges. Your students will never learn anything about writing that does not fit into one of these

Canons. While they do not master these tools during LTW I, they do practice using them, and they learn that every writer uses the tools of the craft, not only the mysteriously gifted. The rest of their writing careers will be devoted to mastery.

PART TWO
Sequence & Schedules: A Proposed Plan of Action

Now that we have introduced the basics of what you will be teaching in The Lost Tools of Writing™, this chapter proposes a sequence and schedule by which you can teach this material.

The next few pages will detail how to use our Three-week Essay Sequence and Year-At-A-Glance chart, organized so that every lesson can be taught in three-week segments.

As you prepare to teach *The Lost Tools of Writing*™, remember that this curriculum should be integrated with your other studies, including literature, history, or even Bible, government, and economics. Literature provides the most straight-forward plan since we offer so many literary examples. But you can and should use these tools with other subjects as well. Don't hesitate to have students ask questions, create issues, work through the Common Topics, and even write extra essays related to a historical event, a key moment in scientific discovery, your study of governmental systems, and more. This is a thinking, reading, and writing program, so it can be applied to a wide range of options.

Important Planning Principles

- ❖ Teach one canon at a time. Beginning writers need to learn separately the tools of discovering (Invention), ordering (Arrangement), and expressing (Elocution).

- ❖ Plan for discussion, contemplation, and revision. The benefits are immeasurable.

- ❖ Coach your students. Help them understand the lesson, guide their practice, encourage them when they falter, and praise them when they succeed.

- ❖ Relish your students' accomplishments. Sometimes we need to pause and enjoy what we have learned.

- ❖ Take your time on the basics. Shortcuts lead to long delays. You are teaching foundational skills, so don't neglect modeling, practicing, and reviewing the fundamentals.

- ❖ Remember the big picture. You are training students to discover and communicate ideas with beauty, propriety, order, and grace, and, even better, you are cultivating wisdom.

THE THREE-WEEK ESSAY SEQUENCE

The Lost Tools of Writing™ follows a three-week sequence. Each essay (which includes one lesson from each of the three canons) takes three weeks and assumes either that you will meet with your students twice weekly or that they will complete the required work independently if you meet only once each week. Try to complete one essay every three weeks, but do not feel compelled to complete lessons that your students have not learned.

If you can meet more than twice a week, take full advantage. Use the additional classes to complete unfinished lessons, deepen your students' understanding, and supervise their work. Practice what they are learning with additional issues, extra writing practice, and especially in-class discussions. Students progress more rapidly when a coach frequently reviews and encourages them to refine their work. They also progress when they see the tools being used in surprising contexts.

After completing the Introductory Lesson, you will follow the three-week sequence nine times. With this pattern, *The Lost Tools of Writing*™ *Level One* provides material for 28 weeks of instruction.

You *might* be able to accelerate the pace if you have older or more experienced students, or if you can meet with your students more than twice weekly. The flexibility of *The Lost Tools of Writing*™ enables you to respond to your students' readiness and experiences.

But before you hurry, meditate on these words from St. John of Kronstadt:

> *Unfortunate is he who loves haste; he will meet with*
> *a multitude of annoying obstacles, and he will fume inwardly;*

through his desire for haste he will be irritated time without number.

It can be humbling to admit this, but sometimes our haste as teachers inoculates our students against what we want them to learn because it leads to irritation and fuming—and that not always inwardly! It would be much better to thoroughly learn five lessons than to be frustrated by ten.

THE ESSAYS IN SEQUENCE
This table illustrates the three-week sequence.

Three-Week Lesson Sequence

	MONDAY	TUESDAY	WEDNESDAY	THURSDAY
WEEK 1	**Invention Lesson**	Apply Invention to practice essay and current essay	Complete Invention Return and discuss prior lesson's essays	Review Invention & Make corrections to prior lesson's essays
WEEK 2	**Arrangement Lesson**	Sort ANI & Complete Worksheets	Imitate Template	Apply Elocution edits to essays
WEEK 3	**Elocution Lesson** Convert outlines into essays	Apply Elocution edits to essays & Refine essays	Discuss & Collect essays	Review and relax

EXPLANATION OF THE THREE-WEEK LESSON SEQUENCE
This assumes Monday and Wednesday classes. Monday and Thursday also work well.

WEEK ONE

On Monday, present the Invention lesson. This usually involves teaching your students a new topic and showing them how to use it. Do not force yourself to complete this lesson if time is tight.

On Tuesday, students should practice what they learned in Monday's class. This usually means applying that week's Topic of Invention.

Wednesday's class consists of the second Invention discussion. Either complete the lesson from Monday or review all Invention to date.

Also on Wednesday, return the previous lesson's essays (beginning with Lesson Two). Discuss the essays with the writers. Let them know if they performed the new skills correctly and how to fix errors. See *Appendix B: A Guide to Assessment,* for details on how to evaluate your students' writing.

Draw your students' attention to common errors in grammar, punctuation, mechanics, etc., assuming that they come from misunderstanding and not vice.

For homework **on Thursday and Friday**, your students will practice all Invention skills and concepts learned to date. They will finish the Invention process and assemble their materials for class on Monday. Finally, they will make corrections to the essays you returned on Wednesday.

WEEK TWO

The following Monday, teach the new Arrangement lesson. Each Arrangement lesson teaches one new element of the persuasive essay. Each Arrangement exercise involves four steps. Your students will do the following:

- *Sort the Invention materials (they will skip this in Lesson One)*
- *Learn and practice a new essay part*
- *Complete the Arrangement worksheet*
- *Imitate the Arrangement template*

Every Arrangement lesson except the second involves one class session. During Essay Two, you will use one Arrangement class to teach how to sort the Invention materials and another to teach how to complete the worksheets and templates. Samples of every worksheet and template can be found in the appendices to this Teacher's Guide and in the Student Workbook.

On Tuesday your students will complete all or part of the four steps listed above. Instruct your students to complete these steps separately.

On Wednesday, in class, you will review the completed Arrangement work, and complete any remaining parts.

In most cases, your students will learn these skills in class, and then apply them to their essays on their own.

For homework on **Thursday and Friday**, your students convert their outlines into essays (a first draft) and then bring them to class on Monday.

WEEK THREE

On Monday your students bring their first drafts to class, during which you introduce the Elocution lesson. The Elocution lessons will teach the following:

- *Basic editing*
- *Schemes*
- *Tropes*

During this class you might guide your students in a peer review of each other's papers. For this reason, *we do not call the first draft a "rough" draft*. Students often think that means they can bring something rough to class. Certainly you should encourage them to write rough copies with notes, but they will not submit these rough drafts to their peers or to you for review.

During this session you introduce new Elocution tools to your students and show them how to add them to their drafts.

On Tuesday, your students will refine their papers before submitting them to you on Wednesday. Make yourself available to your students on this day. Your students should incorporate into their essays any revisions, insights, or new materials added in Monday's class.

On Wednesday, discuss your students' essays, answer their questions (*cherish the questions you do not have answers for*), review the lessons of the past three weeks, and collect the essays. If time permits, consider having students read their essays to each other in small groups, to the whole class, or both.

ADAPTATIONS FOR A ONCE A WEEK CLASS

Many teachers and parents have used the *Lost Tools of Writing*™ meeting once weekly.

Here are few tips to adapt the lesson plan explained above:

1. Keep the three-week cycle, if possible; expand as necessary.

2. Aim to teach one Canon (lesson) each week.

3. Plan homework carefully and realistically. Your students should be practicing the ideas and skills at home after you have coached them in class.

4. Provide clear take-home instructions for students and parents.

5. Adapt homework and expectations as needed. If students do not understand an idea in class or while doing their homework, give it more time.

6. Help students take responsibility to complete the worksheets quickly after each class (to increase retention), to use the essay checklists provided, to reference the glossary, and to ask questions before work is due.

7. Keep the planning simple:
    a. Week 1- Teach the Invention Lesson in class. Assign the Invention worksheet and the new ANI/Invention work for homework.
    b. Week 2: Teach the Arrangement lesson in class. Try to complete the new Arrangement Lesson worksheet together. Assign the Essay Worksheet and Template for homework.
    c. Week 3: Teach the Elocution lesson in class. Practice the new scheme or trope together. Make sure students are ready to write the first draft and assign that for homework. Remind students to use the essay checklist and complete a well-done first draft.
    d. The next Week 1: Renew the cycle again with Invention. You will also collect the last essay. As you repeat this cycle, give yourself time to find the balance between new work, grading, and discussion time. Don't overdo it for yourself or your students.

THE YEAR-AT-A-GLANCE CHART

The Year-at-a-Glance table on the following pages illustrates the full sequence for the nine essays of *The Lost Tools of Writing*™ Level One. Notice that each column represents what you will teach in each *essay* while the rows represent the material for each *Canon*.

By following the lesson sequence included in the chart, you will fulfill the immediate goals of the first year of *The Lost Tools of Writing*™:

- ❖ To introduce the student to the three Canons of classical composition.

- ❖ To practice each Canon with ever-increasing skill and depth of insight.

Points to remember:

- ❖ A cycle is one essay.

- ❖ Every essay (if you follow the schedule recommended in this chapter) takes three weeks to teach.

- ❖ It is not necessary to follow this sequence and schedule like a law book; allow for some flexibility in your teaching.

YEAR-AT-A-GLANCE CHART: PART 1

	Week 1	Weeks 2-4	Weeks 5-7	Weeks 8-10	Weeks 11-13	Weeks 14-16	Weeks 17-19
	Intro	Essay 1	Essay 2	Essay 3	Essay 4	Essay 5	Essay 6
INVENTION	Introduction to the Canons of classical composition	**Invention 1** The "ANI" Chart	**Invention 2** Introduction to the Five Common Topics	**Invention 3** Comparison: Similarities	**Invention 4** Comparison: Differences in Degree & Kind	**Invention 5** Definition	**Invention 6** Circumstance
ARRANGEMENT	Introduction to the Canons of classical composition	**Arrangement 1** Rudimentary Persuasive Essay: From ANI to Outline	**Arrangement 2A** Sorting **Arrangement 2B** Outline	**Arrangement 3** Exordium	**Arrangement 4** Amplification	**Arrangement 5** Division & Distribution	**Arrangement 6** Refutation
ELOCUTION	Introduction to the Canons of classical composition	**Elocution 1** Outline to Text	**Elocution 2** Scheme: Parallelism 1	**Elocution 3** Basic Editing: Verbs	**Elocution 4** Scheme: Parallelism 2	**Elocution 5** Scheme: Antithesis	**Elocution 6** Trope I: Similes

YEAR-AT-A-GLANCE CHART: PART 2

Weeks 20-22	Weeks 23-25	Weeks 26-28
Essay 7	Essay 8	Essay 9
Invention 7 Relation	**Invention 8** Testimony	**Invention 9** Complete Invention Review
Arrangement 7 Narratio	**Arrangement 8** Complete Persuasive Essay: Review & Practice	**Arrangement 9** Complete Persuasive Essay: Review & Practice
Elocution 7 Scheme: Alliteration	**Elocution 8** Trope: Metaphor	**Elocution 9** Scheme: Assonance

PART THREE
Introducing the Lesson Guides

In Parts One and Two we introduced you to the three canons of classical composition (Invention, Arrangement, and Elocution), and to the sequence and schedule of The Lost Tools of Writing™. Here you meet the lesson guides, learning their purpose and structure and how best to use them. To see a more detailed description of the lessons, see Appendix H: Essay Summaries.

Each lesson lays a foundation for the following lessons. Your students will not be able to proceed to the next skill or idea without a solid understanding of the skills and ideas of previous lessons.

Each lesson guide has corresponding worksheets in the Student Workbook.

THE PURPOSE, STRUCTURE, & ORDER OF THE GUIDES

The Lost Tools of Writing™ Level One is divided into nine essays, so this teacher's guide is divided into nine essay guides, and each essay is divided into three separate lessons—one for each Canon. In every essay guide there is an Invention lesson, an Arrangement lesson, and an Elocution lesson (the only exceptions to this rule are the Introductory and Review essays – the first and last).

You will find the lesson guides beginning on page 29.

The guides consist of six elements:
1. Definitions
2. Background information for the teacher
3. Examples
4. Steps to teach the lesson
5. How to assess the lesson
6. Sample worksheet, template, or essay

Please note:
Assessment is explained in detail in Appendix B: *A Guide to Assessment.*

THE CONTENT OF ESSAYS ONE THROUGH NINE

Overviews of each of the lessons follow. You can approach them in one of two ways: You may read all of them in succession to gain a closer overview than you have received so far. Or, you may read them one at a time in order to prepare for your current lesson.

Essay 1: Rudimentary Persuasive Essay

In the first essay cycle your students will learn how to write a Rudimentary Persuasive Essay (RPE). They will learn:

- **Invention: ANI** *How to discover affirmative, negative, and interesting facts about an issue and record these facts in a three-column chart called the ANI*

- **Arrangement: Thesis and Outline** *How to generate a thesis statement and how to turn the ANI into an outline with three proofs*

- **Elocution:** *How to convert the outline into an essay consisting of sentences and paragraphs*

Essay 2: Introductory Persuasive Essay

In the second essay cycle your students **will begin a new essay, with a new issue.** They learn how to expand the Rudimentary Persuasive Essay to a five-paragraph Introductory Persuasive Essay (IPE) by adding three Sub-Proofs to each main Proof.

- **Invention: Topics** *Students will learn* **the Five Common Topics**. *You will teach these topics in the remaining essays, thus enabling your students to practice them with increasing effectiveness*

- **Arrangement: Sorting** *How to sort the information they gathered under Invention and then use the sorted information to expand their Proofs with Sub-Proofs*

- **Elocution: Parallelism 1** *How to write words in the same grammatical pattern*

Essay 3: Introductory Persuasive Essay

In the third essay cycle your students start with a new issue and ANI, continue to expand their essays with tools from each Canon, and refine the essay with an Exordium.

- **Invention: Comparison I** *Students refine their understanding of the Common Topic of Comparison to discover the similarities between two terms and add what they discover to their ANI charts*

- **Arrangement: Exordium** *Students learn to add an Exordium to the essay outline. The Exordium opens the essay by relating the essay's idea to the audience*

- **Elocution: Verbs** *Students learn to find and revise vague and imprecise verbs so they can energize their sentences while also writing more clearly and precisely*

Essay 4

In the fourth essay cycle your students once again write on a new issue, generating additional detail and further refining the essay with an Amplification.

- **Invention: Comparison 2** *Students gather information using the topic of Comparison to discover differences of degree (how much?) and kind (what kind?)*

- **Arrangement: Amplification** *Students learn how to generate and add an Amplification to the conclusion of the essay outline. An Amplification closes the essay by answering the questions, "Who cares?" and "why?"*

- **Elocution: Parallelism 2** *Students learn how to write phrases and clauses with parallelism*

Essay 5

In this essay cycle your students write their fifth persuasive essay, using a new issue and all the tools previously learned. Adding a Division, they begin to respond to the positions of those who disagree with them.

- **Invention: Definition** *Students learn how to gather information using the Common Topic of Definition by identifying the group to which a term belongs and how it is different from other members of the same group*

- **Arrangement: Division** *Students will learn how to generate and add Division, which highlights the precise point of disagreement between a writer and his "opponents"*

- **Elocution: Antithesis** *Students will learn how to generate contrasting ideas in parallel form*

Essay 6

In the sixth essay cycle your students write their sixth persuasive essay, adding tools from each of the three Canons.

- **Invention: Circumstance** *Students will learn how to gather information by asking what is happening at the same time as and in different places from the situation in which the decision needs to be made*

- **Arrangement: Refutation** *Students will learn how to generate and add the Refutation to their essay. The refutation presents the arguments from the opposite position and shows where they are weak. It is easily and conveniently developed from the sorted ANI*

- **Elocution: Simile** *Students will learn how to generate similes and add them to the essay*

Essay 7

In the seventh essay cycle your students write their seventh persuasive essay, their first Complete Persuasive Essay (CPE), because it is the first essay to include all the essay elements.

- **Invention: Relation** *Students will learn how to gather information using the topic of Relation by looking at events occurring before and after* *the time of the issue*

- **Arrangement: Narratio** *Students will learn how to generate and add a statement of facts to the persuasive essay outline. Narratio tells the background story of the events that led to the issue*

- **Elocution: Alliteration** *Students will learn how to generate alliteration and add it to the essay*

Essay 8

In the eighth essay cycle your students will write their eighth Persuasive Essay, reviewing the elements of the essay and adding tools for Invention and Elocution.

- **Invention: Testimony** *Students will learn how to gather information using the Topic of Testimony by gathering the reports of witnesses*

- **Arrangement: CPE** *Students review all of the essay parts and generate a Complete Persuasive Essay template*

- **Elocution: Metaphor** *Students will learn how to generate metaphors and add them to the essay*

Essay 9

In the ninth essay cycle you summarize and apply what your students have learned throughout *The Lost Tools of Writing Level One* and teach one more Elocution tool.

- **Elocution: Assonance** *Students will learn how to generate assonance and add it to the essay*

THE LESSON GUIDES

The Introductory Lesson
THE THREE WRITING CHALLENGES

The Introductory Lesson differs from every other lesson in *The Lost Tools of Writing*™. For one thing, it only takes one week or two classes. For another, everything that follows in lessons one through nine is based on this lesson.

CONTEXT

The Lost Tools of Writing™ is not a collection of new inventions or technologies, but of tools that your students have been using since even before they could read. They arise from human nature and are used in every imaginable context. Consequently, your students will learn names for things they already know, they will refine their use of those tools, and they will come to use those tools and ideas more effectively both in academics and in real life.

The Introductory Lesson equips you to help your students see and name things they already know. It also shows them that when they write they confront the same challenges every other writer has, from William Shakespeare to the classmate beside them.

Discovering that there are only three challenges for the writer is a great relief to most students, for whom writing is a rather mysterious process. When they see that you understand and can provide solutions to these challenges, their confidence increases – along with their readiness for the subsequent lessons.

TEACHER'S PREPARATION

The Introductory Lesson introduces the program through a teacher-led discussion about the *three challenges in writing*.

To prepare the Introductory Lesson, make sure you are familiar with the three Canons. Remember that there are three challenges in writing and that the three Canons solve those challenges (see Part One of this Introduction for more detail):

1. **Invention** solves the challenge of coming up with something to say.
2. **Arrangement** solves the challenge of ordering your thoughts.
3. **Elocution** solves the challenge of expressing your thoughts appropriately.

TEACHING THE INTRODUCTORY LESSON: CHALLENGES COLLECTED

Ask for three volunteers who will record what students say on the white boards.

Then ask your students what they find challenging when they write. Do not hurry. If they aren't used to a class discussion, they might be concerned with offering the "right" answer. Ask them questions to encourage thinking and conversation. *What challenges come to mind when they are assigned an essay? What might trip them up if you asked them to start writing now? What takes the most time when they write?* Some students might find it easier to write something before saying it, so you could also ask them each to write three things they find challenging. Then ask class members to share one of the things on their list. Let the conversation go from there.

As they answer, instruct the volunteers to record each problem on one of the three boards. Students will tell you their challenges, and you will tell the volunteers where to write them. Do not label the boards yet.

On the first board: *Challenges related to Invention*
i.e. thinking up something to say, coming up with a thesis, etc.

On the second board: *Challenges related to Arrangement*
i.e. ending the text, putting your thoughts in order, etc.

On the third board: Challenges related to *Elocution*
i.e. coming up with the right word, figuring out the best sentence pattern, etc.

Some problems will go on more than one board. For example, coming up with an opening is related to both Invention and Arrangement.

If one student says, "I can't come up with anything to say," that goes on the first board. If another says, "I don't know when I am done," that goes on the second board. If a third says, "I can't find just the right word," that goes on the third board.

If you are unsure where something goes, don't be afraid to say so. Your students will be more willing to learn if they see that willingness in you. Suggest a board that it seems to go on. Or, put it on the side for a moment. It will probably become clear through discussion.

Once you have collected at least a few (preferably ten or more) examples of challenges for each Canon, you can begin to compare what your students have told you.

Note: Some students will report subjective problems like being bored, frustrated, unmotivated. When they do so, redirect them to the objective side by asking them what they are bored, frustrated, or unmotivated about. Tell them that these problems disappear when they apply the solutions to the objective problems of writing.

CHALLENGES COMPARED AND IDENTIFIED

When you finish this discussion, guide the students in a comparison of what they have listed on the boards. Ask questions like: *"What do these items on the first board have in common?" "How are all these items similar?" "Is there one problem that summarizes everything on this board?"*

When you finish comparing each board, and when you are comfortable that students can tell you in their own words the central idea on each board, then tell them (or ask them) the title for each problem:

> *We meet the challenge of coming up with ideas with 'Invention.'*
>
> *We meet the challenge of getting our ideas in order with 'Arrangement.'*
>
> *We meet the challenge of expressing our ideas fittingly with 'Elocution.'*
>
> *In each class we will learn a new tool that enables us to overcome these challenges: the tools of Invention, Arrangement, and Elocution.*

CHALLENGES MET

You can end with a simple promise like this:

> *This entire year is devoted to solving the three challenges you have identified today. If we can overcome these three challenges, we can all write well. And you can. So you will.*

ESSAY ONE

Essay One Invention
FROM ISSUE TO ANI

Tools For the Teacher

Invention One Worksheet: The ANI chart (Student Workbook pg. 3)
Samples from this lesson guide for class discussion

Definitions

- ❖ **Issue:** A question converted to a whether statement. The Issue serves to generate questions about both the affirmative and negative responses to the question. Students generate a new Issue for each new essay.

Background for the Teacher

- ❖ **Idea:** Through Essay One: Invention your students learn to respond to stories by asking whether an action should be or should have been done and to gather information for and against that action. They will collect the information on a three-column ANI chart, which stands for Affirmative, Negative, and Interesting.

- ❖ **Why do we start with a "should" question?**
  When your students ask a "should" question, they begin to examine the propriety of a character's actions. Stories, like life, turn on decisions and actions. So the "should" question takes the reader into the heart of the story.

  Furthermore, LTW teaches classical rhetoric, and rhetoric concerns itself with decision-making and persuasion. By teaching your students to ask questions about characters they are reading about and to use powerful tools to answer those questions, you both introduce them to the art of rhetoric and equip them with decision-making tools they can use throughout their lives.

❖ **How do I know it's a good "should" question or issue?**
Don't worry about it! If you and your students ask whether a character should have done something, you will find yourselves reading the story closely, even if you choose a minor action by a marginal character. But let's say, for some reason, a given question does not work for your student. Simply generate a new "should" question. Remember, you can ask about any action by any character.

Your Students Will Learn to:

✓ Ask a "should" question.
✓ Turn the question into an issue using the cue word "whether."
✓ Complete an ANI chart.

Steps to Teach the Lesson

☐ Your students already constantly ask "should" questions, so this lesson is not as new as they might think. Help them realize this – and increase their comfort with the lesson – by asking them about decisions they have made in the last day, week, or month. Simple questions like, "Why did you come to school? Should you have?" "What are you wearing? Should you be?" "What are you eating for lunch? Why?" etc., make excellent examples.

After you have collected a few decisions (all of which boil down to whether something should be done), ask your students to describe how they made them. Draw their attention to their use of reasons for (affirmative) and against (negative).

Note that you are not yet presenting the lesson; you are showing them that it isn't as entirely new and irrelevant as they might have thought. Indeed, you are about to show them how to better use tools they already use in their lives to write an essay.

☐ To show students how to generate an Issue and an ANI chart, **model and practice** the process with them using multiple examples. Several samples are provided below. Generate additional questions from your own reading and that of your students. Fairy Tales, fables, folk tales, myths, Bible Stories, short stories, novels, literature and/or historical narratives all work well – as does any story that involves a decision.

- Select a story source. We have generated examples from *The Lion, the Witch and the Wardrobe,* "*The Gift of the Magi,*" the *Iliad,* and "*The King and His Hawk.*" Any story will do.

- Generate one "should" question about a character from your source and show the question to your students in this form:

    Should _____(character) have (or do) _____(action)?

- Show your students how to convert each "should" question into an Issue by moving the word "should" after the character and adding the word "Whether" to the beginning:

    Whether _____ (character) should have _____(action).

- Complete an ANI chart by generating reasons why this action should (A column) or should not (N column) have been done.

    o *The A column is for affirmative reasons.*
    o *The N column is for negative reasons.*
    o *The I column is for any other interesting but not clearly A or N ideas that come up during your thinking.*

☐ **Practice** completing ANI charts as many times as needed by generating a new question, converting it to an Issue, and arguing for and against the Issue.

☐ **Review** this lesson by asking students to compare what they did each time they completed the process. The following questions help guide them to the idea: *"What type of question did you start with each time? How did you turn that question into an issue? How did you complete the ANI chart?"*

☐ **Assign** the Invention Worksheet, page 3 in the Student Workbook

- Depending on the ability and needs of your students, you can either select a common Issue for the whole class, or each student can generate his own Issue. In either case, they must complete the ANI chart.

> **Teaching Tip**
> The issue is not the thesis, as no one has picked a side yet, but it expresses the question that leads to the thesis. Remember that the word "whether" serves as our cue to **think** about the question from both sides.

- You should decide how many items students must add to each column of the ANI chart in Lesson One, but remember that this is the first of many ANIs. Asking students to find 10 A's, 10 N's, and a few I's usually works very well for the first ANI. You'll be delighted to see how much they generate in later lessons when teaching them the Topics of Invention – and so will they!

Examples

Example A
from The Lion, the Witch, and the Wardrobe

- ❖ **Should Question:** *Should Edmund have followed the White Witch?*
- ❖ **Issue:** *Whether Edmund should have followed the White Witch*

AFFIRMATIVE	NEGATIVE	INTERESTING
She was pretty	Lucy had warned him WW was evil	She had a sled
He was cold		A dwarf was with her
She had candy	She was mean to the dwarf	It was winter
Promised him power	She looked mean sometimes	Edmund was lost
Edmund was lost	She wasn't kind to her horses	Edmund is staying with a professor
She was nice to him	She yelled at Edmund	
She was queen	She scared Edmund	Children were bored
She knows her way in Narnia	She only gave him Turkish Delight when she wanted something from him	Playing hide and go seek
She took care of him		Ed has brother Peter
She tells him they are in Narnia	He acted in secret	Sister Lucy
	He snuck away	Sister Susan
	He lied to his siblings about seeing WW	Witch was tall
	He left Lucy and the Beavers	

Example B
from "The Gift of the Magi"

❖ **Should question:** *Should Della cut her hair?*

❖ **Issue:** *Whether Della should cut her hair*

AFFIRMATIVE	NEGATIVE	INTERESTING
Only way she can afford a gift	Need other things more	It's Christmas
She has something of value	She does have some money	Live in NYC
Big gesture = great love	Jim wears shabby clothes	What's a flat?
Extravagant	Jim needs a coat	Gray cat sounds depressing
Willing to sacrifice	Too emotional to make big decision	What's a pier glass?
Jim is worth it	Not a wise decision	She is cooking chops
He needs to look professional	Jim might not like her with short hair	I wonder if she ever cut her hair before?
Sacrificed her chance at the combs	Permanent decision	Magi = 3 wise men
Wanted to make Jim happy	There are cheaper gifts	Jim works hard
Would look cute with short hair	Needs to be patient	Della loves Jim

Example C
from The King and His Hawk

- ❖ **Should question:** *Should Genghis Kahn have killed his hawk?*
- ❖ **Issue:** *Whether Genghis Kahn should have killed his hawk*

AFFIRMATIVE	NEGATIVE	INTERESTING
Genghis Kahn was an emperor	Pets are companions	Genghis Kahn is a man
Could use feathers for a hat	Hawk was protective	He was a warrior
Genghis Kahn was mean	Good sense of smell to detect danger	They were going home
The hawk saved him	Felt grief	Hawks have excellent vision
Guilt produced a change in him	They were friends	Genghis Kahn was a feared ruler
Made him feel powerful	Hawk could help him find food	Genghis Kahn was separated from his hunting party
He could eat the bird	Hawk is a living thing	They did not have a good hunt
He could have died of thirst	Unsportsmanlike	
He couldn't see the snake	Found a poisonous snake	
No one should disrespect the king for any reason	Hawk saved his life	
	Waste of good hawk training	

Assessment
Confirm that students have:

- ✓ Correctly converted a question to an Issue
- ✓ Completed the ANI chart

SAMPLE STUDENT WORKSHEET

Essay One Invention
THE ANI CHART

Write your Issue.

_____

Fill out the form below.

AFFIRMATIVE (A)	NEGATIVE (N)	INTERESTING (I)

Essay One Arrangement
FROM ANI TO OUTLINE

Tools for The Teacher

Arrangement One Worksheet (Student Workbook pg. 4)
Arrangement One Template (Student Workbook pg. 6)
Samples from this lesson guide for class discussion

Definitions

- **Introduction**
  The opening of the essay, developed after the student has developed the Proof and the Conclusion

- **Conclusion**
  The ending of the essay, developed after the Proof and before the Introduction

- **Thesis**
  The proposition defended by the essay

- **Enumeration**
  The number of reasons used to support the Thesis statement

- **Exposition**
  A statement of the main Proofs in the essay

- **Arrangement Template**
  The pattern on which the outline is modeled; the structure of the essay in outline form

- **Worksheet**
  In this curriculum, a worksheet is a form that guides the students through a thought-pattern so they can imitate it. When students internalize the thought-pattern, the worksheet is no longer needed.

Background for the Teacher

- ❖ **Idea:** You form your Thesis statement by picking a side, A or N, and converting the issue to an affirmative or negative statement.

- ❖ **Skills:** Students will learn to generate a simple outline that includes the rudimentary parts of an essay (the Rudimentary Persuasive Essay Outline: RPE)

- ❖ **Why are students required to write such a simple outline?**
  By generating an RPE, students easily master the essential, foundational essay parts. They learn the elements and how to order them in a simple structure that subsequent lessons build upon. Finally, they prepare for later lessons, as the challenges of those lessons would not be manageable without this solid structure.

Students Will Learn to:

- ✓ Write a Thesis statement
- ✓ Select proofs from the A and N columns to support the Thesis
- ✓ Use the Arrangement Worksheet to order their ANI materials
- ✓ Use the RPE template to create a Rudimentary Outline

Steps to Teach the Lesson

☐ To help students realize how universal structure and form are, start with a brief discussion on a well-known structure or form, such as the field a game is played on, the framing of a house, or a skeleton.

You might ask questions like, "What would happen if... you tried to build a house without a frame, or a bookcase was made like a table, or the basketball hoops were put underground?"

Other questions you might use include, "Can X fit in Y?" (e.g. Can an elephant fit in a mouse's skeleton?) How would you feel if…(e.g. somebody moved the goal posts as you kicked a field goal?)

Ask simple questions that help your students see that everything has its own unique structure and that, in most cases, if you change the structure you either destroy or change the thing.

☐ To show your students how to generate an outline from the ANI chart, model and practice the process with them using multiple examples. Several are provided below. You should also generate examples from your own reading.

- *Refer to a completed ANI chart, one either from the first Invention lesson or quickly generated for this discussion.*
- *Pick three compelling reasons (Proofs) for each side from the A and N columns.*
- *Choose a side to defend.*
- *Write a Thesis statement.*
    - *Restate the Issue as a statement representing the affirmative or negative position.*
- *Complete Arrangement Worksheet 1*
    - *Be sure to explain the new essay terms as you complete this worksheet and the following template together.*
- *Generate a very simple (Rudimentary) outline following the pattern on Template One. Demonstrate how to move the information from the worksheet onto the outline.*

> **Teaching Tip**
> Depending on the ability and needs of your class, they should either complete the worksheet and outline independently or complete the lesson together.

☐ Review this lesson by asking your students to compare what they did each time they completed the process.
"How did you generate a Thesis statement each time? How did you defend it? Where did your proofs come from each time? In what order did you generate the parts of the outline? How did you reorder them to match the template?"

☐ Assign the Essay One Worksheet and Rudimentary Template (Page 4 in the Student Workbook) for the student's current Issue.

Examples

Example A
from The Lion, the Witch, and the Wardrobe

❖ **Issue:** *Whether Edmund should have followed the White Witch*

AFFIRMATIVE	NEGATIVE	INTERESTING
She was pretty	Lucy had warned him WW was evil	She had a sled
He was cold		A dwarf was with her
She had candy	She was mean to the dwarf	It was winter
Promised him power	She looked mean sometimes	Edmund was lost
Edmund was lost	She wasn't kind to her horses	Edmund is staying with a professor
She was nice to him	She yelled at Edmund	Children were bored
She was queen	She scared Edmund	
She knows her way in Narnia	She only gave him Turkish Delight when she wanted something from him	Playing hide and go seek
She took care of him		Ed has brother Peter
She tells him they are in Narnia	He acted in secret	Sister Lucy
	He snuck away	Sister Susan
	He lied to his siblings about seeing WW	Witch was tall
	He left Lucy and the Beavers	

✓ *Select three compelling reasons (proofs) for the A and N columns.*
✓ *Choose a side.*
✓ *Write a thesis statement.*
✓ *Complete Arrangement Worksheet 1.*
✓ *Write an outline using the form of Arrangement Template 1.*

❖ **Sample Outline**

I. Introduction
    A. Edmund should not have followed her
    B. 3 reasons
    C. Exposition
        1. Ignored a warning
        2. Overlooked the evil
        3. Acted in secret

II. Proof
    A. Ignored a warning
    B. Overlooked the evil
    C. Acted in secret

III. Conclusion
    A. Thesis: Edmund should not have followed the White Witch
    B. Summary of Proof
        1. Ignored a warning
        2. Overlooked the evil
        3. Acted in secret

Example B
from The Gift of the Magi

❖ **Issue:** *Whether Della should cut her hair*

❖ **Sample ANI**

AFFIRMATIVE	NEGATIVE	INTERESTING
It's the only way she can afford a gift	Need other things more	It's Christmas
She has something of value	She does have some money	Live in NYC
Big gesture = great love	Jim wears shabby clothes	What's a flat?
Extravagant	Jim needs a coat	Gray cat sounds depressing
Willing to sacrifice	Too emotional to make big decision	What's a pier glass?
Jim is worth it	Not a wise decision	She is cooking chops

He needs to look professional	Jim might not like her with short hair	I wonder if she ever cut her hair before?
Sacrificed her chance at the combs	Permanent decision	Magi = 3 wise men
Wanted to make Jim happy	There are cheaper gifts	Jim works hard
Would look cute with short hair	Needs to be patient	Della loves Jim

- ✓ Select three compelling reasons (proofs) for the A and N columns.
- ✓ Choose a side.
- ✓ Write a Thesis statement.
- ✓ Complete Arrangement Worksheet 1.
- ✓ Write an outline using the form of Arrangement Template 1.

❖ Sample Outline

I. Introduction
    A. Della should cut her hair.
    B. 3 reasons
    C. Exposition
        1. sacrifice
        2. love
        3. Christmas

II. Proof
    A. sacrifice
    B. love
    C. Christmas

III. Conclusion
    A. Della should cut her hair.
    B. Summary of Proof
        1. sacrifice
        2. love
        3. Christmas

Assessment
Confirm that students have:

- ✓ Selected the A or N side
- ✓ Formed a clear, simple Thesis statement
- ✓ Completed Arrangement Worksheet One
- ✓ Imitated Template One to generate a Rudimentary Outline

SAMPLE STUDENT WORKSHEET

Arrangement Template One
RUDIMENTARY PERSUASIVE OUTLINE

Transcribe your outline onto a separate page, imitating the template provided below. Do not use complete sentences.

Replace lines that have an asterisk with your information from the Arrangement Worksheet on the previous pages.

    I. Introduction
        A. *Thesis**

        B. *Enumeration**

        C. *Exposition*
            1. Proof I*
            2. Proof II*
            3. Proof III*

    II. Proof
        A. *Proof 1**

        B. *Proof 2**

        C. *Proof 3**

    III. Conclusion
        A. *Thesis**

        B. *Summary of Proof*
            1. Proof I*
            2. Proof II*
            3. Proof III*

Essay One Elocution
FROM OUTLINE TO ESSAY

Tools for the Teacher

Samples from this lesson guide for class discussion

Definitions

- **Complete Sentence**
  A sentence is a complete thought (a subject, predicate, and correct punctuation).

- **Outline Point**
  A cue or reminder of the information and ideas that become sentences when the students write their essays

Background for the Teacher

- **Idea:** Students will learn how to transform an outline into an essay by converting Arrangement outline points to complete sentences.

- **Why are students required to write such a simple essay?**

The simple form of the Rudimentary Persuasive Essay lays a foundation for every future essay your students will write. To direct their attention to that foundation, this essay remains deliberately simple, exact, and even tedious, which enables students to see clearly its most essential and fundamental parts. In the short term, your students will not be confused about the order of the essay's parts, which promotes confidence. In the long term, they'll build a strong tower on this firm foundation.

If students are concerned about the simplicity of this essay, assure them that this is the only Rudimentary Essay. Each later essay becomes more detailed and complex, which is possible because this structure is strong enough to handle the weight we put on it.

Students Will Learn How To:

✓ Write a Rudimentary Persuasive Essay (RPE) by turning their outline points into sentences and imitating the most basic essay form: Introduction, Proof, and Conclusion.

Steps to Teach the Lesson

☐ To prepare students for this lesson, **review** complete sentences. They should demonstrate their ability to form sentences that express complete thoughts with a subject, verb, and proper punctuation.

Some questions you might ask include:

- *What is a sentence?*
- *What are the parts of a sentence?*
- *What happens when the parts don't agree with each other (e.g. a plural verb goes with a singular subject)?*
- *Can you attach any phrase you want to a sentence?*
- *What happens if it doesn't belong there?*

Show your students outline points from the Arrangement Template and ask whether they are clear and whether they communicate a complete thought.

☐ To teach students how to convert outline points into essay sentences, **practice** the process with them multiple times. Several samples are provided here, and you can and should use additional examples from your own reading.

- *Refer to your outline samples and your students' work from the Essay One Arrangement lesson. Students need to remember the parts of the Rudimentary outline.*
- *Emphasize the role the ANI chart and the outline play when they are challenged to write the essay. They have already completed most (and often the hardest part) of the essay because they have already generated information (Invention) and ordered it (Arrangement). Now they use their outlines to write sentences and form paragraphs.*
- *Show them how to turn the Introduction from the outline into one or two complete sentences in the essay. Note from the samples above that this sentence should include the Enumeration (simply the phrase "three reasons").*
- *Next, turn the Proof from the outline into three sentences in the essay. Students repeat the Thesis with each Proof.*
- *Finally, turn the Conclusion in the outline into a single sentence in the essay. Note that the Enumeration is NOT repeated in the Conclusion.*

☐ As you complete this exercise together, be sure to **review** the new essay terms from the Arrangement One lesson as they arise. Students need to become familiar with the names for the parts of the essay, what those names mean, and where each part goes in the essay.

☐ **Emphasize** with your students that this is the Rudimentary Persuasive Essay. All of them must demonstrate their mastery of this basic form. Although many will be tempted to add more, this RPE demands simplicity and attention to detail. The essay will grow, improve, and become much more interesting with each subsequent lesson.

☐ **Review** by asking your students to compare how they turned outlines into written essays in each model:

- *How did they write the Introduction each time?*
- *How did they write the Proof each time?*
- *How did they write the Conclusion each time?*
- *How will you turn your outline into an essay?*

☐ **Assign** the first essay, the Rudimentary Persuasive Essay.

☐ **Ensure** that students know where the sample essays can be found for reference (page 117 in the Student Workbook) and guide them to the Self-Edit Guide for Essay One on page 107 in the Student Workbook.

Examples

> ### Example A
> *from* The Lion, the Witch, and the Wardrobe

❖ **Issue:** *Whether Edmund should have followed the White Witch*

❖ **Outline**

    I. Introduction
        A. Edmund should not have followed the White Witch
        B. 3 reasons
        C. Exposition
            1. Ignored a warning
            2. Overlooked evil
            3. Acted in secret

    II. Proof
        A. Ignored a warning
        B. Overlooked evil
        C. Acted in secret

III. Conclusion
    A. Edmund should not have followed the White Witch.
    B. Summary of Proof
        1. Ignored a warning
        2. Overlooked evil
        3. Acted in secret

❖ **Sample Rudimentary Persuasive Essay:**

Edmund should not have followed the White Witch for three reasons. Edmund's sister Lucy warned him that the White Witch was evil, he should have seen that the White Witch was evil, and he acted in secret.

The first reason Edmund should not have followed the White Witch was that his sister Lucy warned him that the White Witch was evil. The second reason Edmund should not have followed the White Witch was that he should have seen that the White Witch was evil. The third reason Edmund should not have followed the White Witch was that he acted in secret.

Edmund should not have followed the White Witch because his sister Lucy warned him that the White Witch was evil, he should have seen that the White Witch was evil, and he acted in secret.

Example B
from "The Gift of the Magi"

❖ **Issue:** *Whether Della should cut her hair*

❖ **Outline**

I. Introduction
    A. Della should cut her hair.
    B. 3 reasons
    C. Exposition
        1. sacrifice
        2. love
        3. Christmas

II. Proof
    A. sacrifice
    B. love
    C. Christmas

III. Conclusion
    A. Della should cut her hair.
    B. Summary of Proof
        1. sacrifice
        2. love
        3. Christmas

- **Sample Rudimentary Persuasive Essay:**

  Della should cut her hair for three reasons. She had something she could sacrifice, for love, and it is for Christmas.

  The first reason Della should cut her hair is she had something she could sacrifice. The second reason Della should cut her hair is for love. The third reason Della should cut her hair is it is for Christmas.

  Della should cut her hair because she had something she could sacrifice, for love, and it is for Christmas.

Assessment
Confirm that students have:

- ✓ Correctly written their own Rudimentary Persuasive Essay, referring to the Essay One checklist for self-editing

ESSAY TWO

Essay Two Invention
THE 5 COMMON TOPICS

Tools For the Teacher

Essay Two Invention Worksheet (Page 9 in the Student Workbook)
Samples from this lesson guide for class discussion

Definitions

- **Common Topics**
  The Five Common Topics – Comparison, Definition, Circumstance, Relation, and Testimony – are places we go to gather information, from the Greek word, "topos," meaning place.

- **Interesting Column**
  The column on the ANI chart used to record ideas generated during the Invention process that are not clearly Affirmative or Negative

  All the information students generate during Invention that does not belong to the A or N column should be considered part of the I column, even if they do not copy it onto the chart.

Background for the Teacher

- **Idea:** Students will learn five places writers can go to gather information, known as the Common Topics.

- By learning the names for the Common Topics and using them to generate ideas and content, students learn to use these tools whenever they need them and become acquainted with the language of classical rhetoric.

- At this time, students should become comfortable with the names of the Five Common Topics and the basic questions. Each Topic will be taught in detail in subsequent lessons.

- Remember that the Invention lessons always start a new essay, and the skills learned in previous lessons are practiced again for each new essay. Students begin a new essay by forming a new issue and starting a new ANI.

Your Students Will Learn How to:

- ✓ Use the Five Common Topics to ask questions
- ✓ Record the information generated in the I column of the ANI chart.
- ✓ Review the ideas in the I column to see which can be used to support either the A or N side and move those that can.

Teaching the Five Common Topics

☐ **Show** the class that they already use the questions that make up the Common Topics. Provide a simple issue such as "Whether I should accept an invitation to a certain party" or "Whether I should buy a certain bicycle." Allow and even encourage students to spontaneously ask any questions that come to their minds to gather information to make the decision. Note any that relate to the Common Topics.

☐ To **show** your students how to use the Five Common Topics to generate ideas for an essay, practice the following process with them a few times. Several examples are provided below.

☐ **Begin** a new issue as described in Lesson One.

☐ **Ask students the questions** of the 5 Common Topics to generate ideas for this new ANI together.

- **Topic of Comparison**
    - *How is X similar to Y?*
    - *How is X different from Y?*

- **Topic of Definition**
    - *Who or what is X?*
    - *What kind of thing is X?*

- **Topic of Circumstance**
    - *What was happening in the same place and time as your issue or situation?*
    - *What was happening at the same time as, but in different places from, your issue or situation?*

- **Topic of Relation**
    - *What led to the situation in which a decision needs to be made?*
    - *What followed the decision?*

- **Topic of Testimony**
    - What do witnesses say about the character and/or his actions?

☐ **Show** the students how to move their responses to the Five Common Topics onto their ANI. Those that argue for or against the issue should be moved to the appropriate A or N column. Those that do not should be considered part of the I column.

☐ **Review** this lesson by asking students to compare what they did in each of the examples. Ask:

- *What questions did you ask?*
- *What did you do with that new information?*
- *How will you gather information for your next issue?*

> **Teaching Tip**
>
> As students become familiar with the Common Topics and the worksheets over the following lessons, they will generate many more ideas for the ANI charts.

You might need to clarify the names of the Common Topics as you review the questions.

☐ **Assign** the Essay Two Invention: Common Topics Worksheet (page 9 in the Student Workbook) for their new issue. Depending on the ability and needs of your students, you can either have them complete this worksheet and the ANI chart for an issue common to the whole class (something from your current literature or history studies) or you can ask students to independently form their own issues and complete the ANI chart from that individual issue.

☐ You should **decide** how many items students will add to the ANI chart based on their readiness, but the Essay Two ANIs should be longer than those from Essay One.

Examples

Example A
from The Lion, the Witch, and the Wardrobe

❖ **Issue:** *Whether Edmund should have followed the White Witch*

❖ **Overview of Topics of Invention**

Topic of Comparison

- How is X similar to Y? *Edmund and the White Witch are both in Narnia, both seeking power.*

- How is X different from Y? *Edmund is young and she is older, he is lost and she isn't.*

Topic of Definition

- Who or what is X? *Edmund is one of the four Penvensie children.*

- What kind of thing is Y? *The White Witch is a current ruler of Narnia.*

Topic of Circumstance

- What was happening in the same place and time as your issue or situation? *The dwarf was serving as the White Witch's driver.*

- What was happening at the same time as, but in different places from, your issue or situation? *Many Narnians, like Tumnus, were spies for the White Witch.*

Topic of Relation

- What led to the situation in which a decision needs to be made? *The Witch approached Edmund when he was lost in Narnia.*

- What followed the decision? *Edmund decides to meet the Witch again and she tries to kill him.*

Topic of Testimony

- What do witnesses say about the character and/or his actions? *The Beavers told the Pevensies about the evil actions of the Witch.*

❖ **Show** the students how to move their responses to the Five Common Topics onto their ANI.

AFFIRMATIVE	NEGATIVE	INTERESTING
WW also wanted power	Beavers warned him	Four Pevensie children
WW had experience ruling people	WW employed spies	The dwarf was the WW's driver
WW is older and possibly wiser	Ed had siblings to think of	
Ed was lost and needed help	WW tried to kill him later	

> **Example B**
> *from "The Gift of the Magi"*

❖ **Issue:** *Whether Della should cut her hair*

❖ **Overview of Topics of Invention**

Topic of Comparison

- How is X similar to Y? *Della and Jim are both married, both poor, both live in the city.*

- How is X different from Y? *Jim works at a job, supports a family. Della runs the house.*

Topic of Definition

- Who or what is X? *Della is a young, married woman.*

- What kind of thing is X? *She is his poor wife.*

Topic of Circumstance

- What was happening in the same place and time as your issue or situation? *Shop owners are running their businesses, including buying hair.*

- What was happening at the same time as, but in different places from, your issue or situation? *It's Christmas; Jim is at work.*

Topic of Relation

- What led to the situation in which a decision needs to be made? *No money for a gift, she tries to save money while shopping, their income has been reduced*

- What followed the decision? *Della came home and started to prepare dinner, Jim comes home with his own present.*

Topic of Testimony

- What do witnesses say about the character and/or his actions? *The grocer has seen her penny-pinching.*

❖ **Show** the students how to move their responses to the Five Common Topics onto their ANI.

AFFIRMATIVE	NEGATIVE	INTERESTING
Jim loved her no matter what	Emotional	Christmas highlighted the fact that Della was poor
No money for a gift	Keep saving money at the grocer instead	Della came home and started to prepare dinner
Their income was reduced		
Jim would probably buy her something		
There was a shop to buy hair		

Example C
from "The Nightingale"

❖ **Issue:** *Whether the Japanese Emperor should have sent the mechanical bird to the Chinese Emperor*

❖ **Overview of the Topics of Invention**

Topic of Comparison

- How is X similar to Y? *The mechanical bird and natural Nightingale are both called birds, both have wings, both sing.*

- How is X different from Y? *The mechanical bird is prettier, winds up, and plays limited songs. The nightingale is plain, sings unlimited songs, sings when it chooses, and its song is more beautiful.*

Topic of Definition

- Who or what is X? *The Chinese Emperor is Royal leader, once unaware of real Nightingale, had beautiful kingdom.*
- What is the mechanical bird? *A gift, similar to real bird, not real*

Topic of Circumstance

- What was happening in the same place and time as your issue or situation? *The nightingale was in the court.*

- What was happening at the same time as, but in different places from, your issue or situation? *People were mimicking the Nightingale.*

Topic of Relation

- What led to the situation in which a decision needs to be made? *The emperor of China was given a beautiful gift.*

- What followed the decision? *The two birds sang at the same time, the mechanical bird played on command.*

Topic of Testimony

- What do witnesses say about the character and/or his actions? *Fisherman notes the mechanical bird's song is missing something.*

❖ **Show** the students how to move the information generated by the Five Common Topics onto their ANI.

AFFIRMATIVE	NEGATIVE	INTERESTING
A gift	Not real	Time of emperors
Emperor accepted it	Poor comparison	Emperors contemporaries
Prettier	Song something missing	Kingdom known for Nightingale
Sing on command	Had real one	People copied Nightingale
From contemporary	Limited songs	
Royal gift		

Assessment
Confirm that students have:

✓ Created a new ANI that contains more information in the I column because they used the Five Common Topics

✓ Moved any appropriate ideas from the I column to the A or N columns

SAMPLE STUDENT WORKSHEET

Essay Two Invention
INTRODUCTION TO THE FIVE TOPICS

*The following questions introduce the **Five Common Topics of Invention** that you use whenever you make decisions. You will learn much more about each topic in later lessons. Answers to these questions can be placed in your I column on the ANI chart.*

COMPARISON QUESTIONS
- *How is X similar to Y?*
- *How is X different from Y?*

DEFINITION QUESTIONS
- *Who or what is X?*
- *What kind of thing is X?*

CIRCUMSTANCE QUESTIONS
- *What was happening in the same place and time as your issue or situation?*
- *What was happening at the same time as, but in different places from, your issue or situation?*

RELATION QUESTIONS
- *What led to the situation in which a decision needs to be made?*
- *What followed the decision?*

TESTIMONY QUESTIONS
- *What do witnesses say about the character or his actions?*

Review your I column, and move any appropriate items to the A or N columns.

Essay Two Arrangement
A GUIDE TO SORTING

Tools For the Teacher

Essay Two Arrangement Worksheets and Template (Page 10 in the Student Workbook)
Samples from this lesson guide for class discussion

Definitions

- **Proof:** 1. The body of an essay; it contains the main arguments for the Thesis. 2. The main supports that make up the body of the essay, with the Sub-Proofs, to argue for the Thesis.

- **Sub-Proof:** The supporting reasons or argumentation for the main Proofs of the essay

Background for the Teacher

- **Idea:** Sorting is the process of categorizing the information collected in the ANI chart into groups of related ideas. These groups will be used as proof to support the chosen side of the argument.

- There are many acceptable ways for students to sort the ANI information into groups, and there are many groups into which it can be sorted for any Issue.

- Students will be sorting both the A and the N. The I column is not sorted but continues to provide information and reference in the essay process.

- After sorting, students will give each group a name that identifies what the members of the group share in common. This prepares them to use selected groups as their Proof and Sub-Proofs in the essay.

Your Students Will Learn How to:

- ✓ Sort their Affirmative and Negative information into related groups

- ✓ Choose a side to defend in the Persuasive Essay, either the Affirmative or Negative, based on their groups (proofs for the Thesis)
- ✓ Expand the Rudimentary Persuasive Essay (RPE) Template by adding Sub-Proofs to each Proof, creating the Introductory Persuasive Essay (IPE) Template

---

Steps to Teach Sorting

**<u>Note: Sorting is easy to show and harder to explain on paper.
We cannot urge you energetically enough to watch the video for this lesson.</u>**

☐ Review the Rudimentary Persuasive Template and Essay (this lesson adds to the elements you introduced for Essay One). In particular, review the Thesis statement and three Proofs.

Bring to your students' awareness the process of sorting and its utility in many areas. Even your most disorganized students know the value of sorting various objects into groups. Ask students what they keep sorted in their homes (clothes, books, Legos, silverware, music) and what they see sorted when they go shopping (produce, meats, frozen goods, clothing types, shoes, etc.).

How do you sort those things?
How does this sorting help when you are shopping or finding things in your own home?

☐ To show your students how to sort their ANI charts, practice the sorting steps below several times with your students. Use an ANI that has already been completed.

<u>Sort the A column:</u>

1. Create the first group
    a. Place a symbol by the first item in the A column (do not use numbers as symbols).
    b. Look at the second item in the column and determine whether it can be placed in the same group as the first item. If it can be, place the corresponding symbol next to the item.
    c. Continue down the list and determine which items can be placed in the same group as the first. Mark each with the same symbol.

    You are helping your students to determine whether each item is the same kind of thing as the leading item. If a student thinks two or more items can be joined, they can put them in the same group.

2. Create the Second Group
    a. Return to the second item in the A column and place a different symbol beside it.
    b. Look at each remaining item in the A column to determine whether it can be placed in the same group as the second item. Place the symbol you placed beside the second

item beside each succeeding item that goes with it.

At this point, you can practice one of two types of sorting with your students, depending on their readiness. With Sorting 1, no item can be a member of more than one group. With Sorting 2, items can be placed in an unlimited number of groups.

If your students use sorting 1, they would mark the second item with a new symbol ONLY if it hasn't already been marked as a group-member with the first item.

If they use sorting 2, students are free to sort items into multiple groups, so they can place a new group symbol beside the second item, <u>even if</u> it has already been marked with the symbol of the first group. It has become a member of both groups.

3. Continue creating new groups

   a. Return to the A column.
   b. Place a new symbol by any item that could be the first member of a new group and continue to add additional members.

   Students should form five groups. This gives them options when they choose their three Proofs.

4. Name each group with a fitting heading or summary phrase.

5. Instruct your students to list the group names and the symbols, creating a simple "key."

6. Circle three compelling groups.

   At this point, your students haven't been taught how to determine the most compelling, so they should be free to choose three groups without having to defend their choices.

<u>Sort the items in the N column the same way you sorted the A column.</u>

Your students have not yet taken a side on this issue – they are still examining and ordering the information – so they must sort both columns. Sorting helps make decisions, and the groups generated for both sides will be used in Essay Six: Refutation.

<u>Decide whether you will defend the Affirmative or Negative side.</u> Then form the appropriate Thesis.

<u>List the group names circled above that defend your Thesis.</u> These group names will be used as your Proofs to defend your Thesis.

<u>Select three members that will serve as Sub-Proofs.</u>

☐ Repeat the process of sorting A's and N's with your students several times.

☐ Review sorting by asking your students to compare how they sorted each ANI. *Ask questions like, "How did you create groups for the A column? How did you do it for the N column? How did you name each group? After you selected three groups, where did you find the sub-*

members of each group? How did you decide which side to defend? How will you sort your ANI into groups for your essay?"

☐ **Assign** the Sorting Worksheet (page 10 in the Student Workbook).

☐ After students have practiced the process of sorting with you a couple of times, they are ready for the Essay Two: Arrangement B worksheet. This worksheet takes students through the Order of Essay Development, so the Introduction is *developed* last. This is different than the Order of Presentation (the Template) in which the Introduction is *presented* first.

☐ **Practice** expanding the Template for Essay Two to include three Sub-Proofs for each Proof.

☐ **Review** the new outline by asking your students several questions, such as:

- *How does sorting help develop your essays?*

- *How is the template two the same as template one? How is it different? What part of the essay is developed last? What is developed last? What part is developed first?*

☐ To complete this lesson, students will sort the new ANI that they created in the Essay Two Invention lesson, completing the Arrangement A Guide to Sorting Worksheet, the Essay Two Arrangement B Worksheet, and the Essay Two Template.

Examples

> ### Example A
> *from* The Lion, the Witch, and the Wardrobe

❖ **Issue:** *Whether Edmund should have followed the White Witch*

❖ **Sort the chart below:**

AFFIRMATIVE	NEGATIVE	INTERESTING
* She was pretty @ He was cold @ She had candy & Promised him power # Edmund was lost @ She was nice to him & She was queen # She knows her way in Narnia @ She took care of him # She tells him they are in Narnia @ Turkish Delight is candy that tastes good # She provides shelter in the snow & She was trying to give him what was rightfully his & According to prophecy, he was supposed to rule % It is possible for him to follow her	@ Lucy had warned him WW was evil & She was mean to the dwarf & She looked mean sometimes & She wasn't kind to her horses & She yelled at Edmund & She scared Edmund & She only gave him Turkish Delight when she wanted something from him # He acted in secret # He snuck away # He lied to his siblings about seeing WW # He left Lucy and the Beavers & WW was like Hitler & WW was different from Ed's mother @ Beavers said WW is evil & It's always winter and never Christmas because of WW @ Professor said Lucy didn't lie @ Witches are usually evil in stories.	• She had a sled • A dwarf was with her • It was winter • Edmund was lost • Edmund is staying with a professor • Children were bored • Playing hide and go seek • Ed has brother Peter • Sister Lucy • Sister Susan • Witch was tall • She was pretty • TD is candy • TD has fruit and nuts in it • It was WW II • Kids were staying in the countryside with the professor • London was being bombed • Got into Narnia through the wardrobe playing Hide/Go Seek

Sorted Group Names Affirmative
* WW beauty
# WW knows Narnia
& WW offers power
@ WW helped

Sorted Group Names Negative
@ Lucy warned
# Ed acted in secret
& evil of WW

> **Example B**
> *from* "The Gift of the Magi"

❖ **Issue:** *Whether Della should cut her hair*

❖ **Sort the chart below:**

AFFIRMATIVE	NEGATIVE	INTERESTING
= ! + / It's the only way she can afford a gift	& Need other things more	It's Christmas
+ She has something of value	$ She does have some money	Live in NYC
! + Big gesture = great love	& Jim wears shabby clothes	What's a flat?
! Extravagant	& Jim needs a coat	Gray cat sounds depressing
+ ? / Willing to change looks	* Too emotional to make big decision	What's a pier glass?
^ ! Jim is worth it	* Not a wise decision	She is cooking chops
^ He needs to look professional	% * Jim might not like her with short hair	I wonder if she ever cut her hair before?
? ! + Sacrificed her chance at the combs	* Permanent decision	Magi = 3 wise men
! Wanted to make Jim happy	$ There are cheaper gifts	Jim works hard
? / Would look cute with short hair	* Needs to be patient	Della loves Jim
= God likes cheerful givers	* Prideful	D curled hair after it was cut
= ! + Christmas is a time of gift giving	% Jim will love her if she doesn't buy a gift	She didn't always use proper grammar
= Everyone else giving gifts	% * Jim loves her hair	Good cook
/ Mme. Sofronie is close by	& Should save money for later	Watch chain costs $20
? Long hair is a pain to take care of	% Jim might feel bad about getting a gift paid for with hair	Combs must have been a big deal back then
^ ! Jim needs a chain	@ Hair is too valuable	Coney Island chorus girl - funny way to describe herself
^ Would make him more confident	& Money is scarce	Surprise ending!
= Best surprise	* Shouldn't make big decisions without consulting spouse	King Solomon and Queen of Sheba – rich people
! + Love is more important than things	% $ Short-haired wife might hurt his career	Are possessions the only way to be rich?
	% She would stand out and be	Gray is mentioned 3 times in

74

? Hair grows back = Season of giving = City atmosphere = festive reminders ! Obviously crazy about each other +Permanent decision = ! Chain is perfect gift	odd & $Salary reduction	story Chops mentioned 3 times in story

Sorted Groups–Affirmative
^ Jim's needs
+ Sacrifice
! Love
= Christmas
? Hair issues
/ Opportunity

Sorted Groups – Negative
& Need other things more
% Jim might not like her with short hair
*too emotional
$ cost
@ hair is valuable

Assessment
Confirm that students have:

- ✓ Completed the Sorting Worksheet for their current essay
- ✓ Completed the Essay Two Arrangement B Worksheet
- ✓ Transcribed the Arrangement Two Template for their current essay

SAMPLE STUDENT WORKSHEET

Essay Two Arrangement
A GUIDE TO SORTING

Step One

Sort the items in the A column into groups as follows:

Sort into Group 1

- Place a symbol (such as @ or $) by the first item in the A column.
- Look at the second item in the column, and determine whether it can be placed in the same group as the first item. If it can, place the same symbol next to the second item.
- Review the list, and determine whether each item can be placed in the same group as the first. Mark these with the same symbol.

Sort into Group 2

- Return to the second item in the list, and place a different symbol by it.
- Look at each remaining item in the list to determine whether it can be placed in the same group as the second item. Place the symbol you used for the second item beside each succeeding item that can be included in the same group as the second item.

Keep sorting into new groups

- Review the entire list, placing a new symbol by any item that could be the first member of a new group. Add additional items to each new group. Your goal is to form five groups of related items, all clearly marked with symbols.
- Name each group with a fitting heading or summary phrase.

List these group names below:
1.
2.
3.
4.
5.

Circle the three most compelling groups.

Step Two

Sort the items in the N column as you did in the A column.

- Sort the items into groups with new symbols.
- Name each group with a fitting heading or summary phrase.

List these group names below:
1.
2.
3.
4.
5.

Circle the three most compelling groups.

Step Three

Decide whether you will defend the A or N argument.

Write the Thesis you will defend:

_____

From the side you have chosen to defend, write the group names you circled above. These groups are your Proofs to defend your Thesis.

_____

From the sorting you completed above, list three Sub-Proofs (the members of each group you made) for each Proof:

1a. _____

1b. _____

1c. _____

2a. _____

2b. _____

2c. _____

3a. _____

3b. _____

3c. _____

Essay Two Arrangement Template
INTRODUCTORY PERSUASIVE ESSAY

Transcribe your outline onto a separate page, using the template provided below. Do not use complete sentences.

Replace lines that have an asterisk with your information from the Arrangement Worksheet on the previous pages.

I. Introduction
    A. *Thesis**

    B. *Enumeration**

    C. *Exposition*
        1. Proof I*
        2. Proof II*
        3. Proof III*

II. Proof
    A. *Proof I**
        1. Sub-Proof 1*
        2. Sub-Proof 2*
        3. Sub-Proof 3*
    B. *Proof II**
        1. Sub-Proof 1*
        2. Sub-Proof 2*
        3. Sub-Proof 3*
    C. *Proof III**
        1. Sub-Proof 1*
        2. Sub-Proof 2*
        3. Sub-Proof 3*

III. Conclusion
    A. *Thesis**

    B. *Summary of Proof*
        1. Proof I*
        2. Proof II*
        3. Proof III*

Essay Two Elocution
PARALLELISM I

Tools For The Teacher

Essay Two Elocution Worksheet (page 16 in the Student Workbook)
Samples from this lesson guide for class discussion

Definitions

- **Parallelism:** A similarity of structure in a pair or series of related words, phrases, or clauses (sentences)

Background for the Teacher

- **Idea:** Parallelism is similarity of structure in a pair or series of related words, phrases, or clauses; it gives harmonious form, interest, and beauty to a sentence or passage.

- This lesson focuses on parallel words. Parallel phrases and clauses will be taught in Essay Four Elocution.

Your Students Will Learn to:

- Write their own sentences with parallel word structure

Steps to Teach This Lesson

☐ **Prepare** students for the idea of parallelism by discussing the parallel things they likely already know. What are parallel lines? What is parallel parking? What is parallelism? What does it mean if two things are parallel?

Also, prepare your students to use the parts of speech by ensuring that they know them. This lesson will help them begin to see how practical that knowledge is.

☐ **Present** several models of simple parallelism to your students. You can find several examples below and in the Student Workbook. Remember that this lesson focuses on parallelism of words, and that students will learn to write parallel phrases and clauses in a later lesson.

☐ After reading and discussing the examples, **model** writing with parallelism for your students and then practice this process several times together:

> *Teaching Tip*
> Help your students see the value of parallel word structure and give them time to play with the words. They will form some sentences that sing and some that do not, but guide them through the process in this lesson and encourage them to keep building this writing skill.

- Find a term in your writing that you can expand by adding detail: *Edmund*

- Generate a list of words in the same part of speech as this term: *Lucy, Peter, Tumnus*

- Or list words that relate to your term. List these words by part of speech:

    o *Verb–heed, follow, obey*
    o *Adjective–spoiled, jealous, angry*
    o *Adverb–quickly, submissively, foolishly*

- Select one series of words that are the same part of speech, and add this list as a series to a sentence in your essay. Rewrite the sentence as needed to express a clear, complete thought:

    o *Edmund should heed, follow, and obey the White Witch.*

- Several other possibilities for this example:

    o *Edmund, Lucy, Susan, and Peter are siblings.*
    o *Edmund should not heed, follow, or obey the evil White Witch.*
    o *The spoiled, jealous, angry Edmund considered the White Witch's offer.*
    o *Edmund followed the White Witch quickly, submissively, and foolishly.*

☐ **Repeat** this process with several sentences drawn from your students' work.

☐ **Review** by asking your students to list and describe the steps they took each time they generated a parallel series and added it to a sentence.

- *What did you choose first to begin the process?*
- *What lists did you generate each time? How?*
- *What questions did you ask to generate each list?*
- *How did you change each sentence to include parallelism?*
- *How will you add parallelism to your essays?*

☐ **Assign** the Essay Two Elocution: Parallelism I Worksheet (page 16 in the Student Workbook).

☐ Students will add one or more examples of parallelism to their essays. **Remind** them to refer to the Essay Two checklist to confirm that they have completed their essays.

Examples

- ❖ From Shakespeare's *The Tragedy of Julius Caesar*:

  Friends, Romans, Countrymen, lend me your ears; I come to bury Caesar, not to praise him.

- ❖ From the *Ad Herenium*:

  The Romans destroyed Numantia, razed Carthage, obliterated Corinth, overthrew Fregellae.

- ❖ From Plutarch's life of Julius Caesar:

  I came; I saw; I conquered.

- ❖ From Henry Peacham's *The Garden of Eloquence*:

  He is esteemed eloquent which can invent wittily, remember perfectly, dispose orderly, figure diversely, pronounce aptly, confirm strongly, and conclude directly.

- ❖ From Harper Lee's *To Kill a Mockingbird*:

I understood, pondered a while, and concluded that the only way I could retire with a shred of dignity was to go to the bathroom, where I stayed long enough to make them think I had to go.

❖ William Shakespeare's *Othello:*

Farewell the tranquil mind! Farwell content!
Farewell the plumed troops and the big wars...

Assessment
Confirm that your students have:

- ✓ Completed the Essay Two Elocution: Parallelism One Worksheet
- ✓ Added parallelism to their current essay
- ✓ Written Essay Two, referring to the Essay Two checklist for self-editing

SAMPLE STUDENT WORKSHEET

Essay Two Elocution
PARALLELISM I: WORDS

Definition

Parallelism is similarity of structure in a pair or series of related words, phrases, or clauses (sentences).

Review

List the parts of speech, and provide two or three examples of each.

_____
_____
_____
_____
_____
_____
_____
_____
_____
_____

Steps to Using Parallelism

1. Find a term in your writing that you can expand by adding detail: *Edmund*.

2. Generate a list of words in the same part of speech as this term: *Lucy*.
   Or list words that relate to your term. List these words by part of speech: *verb-heed, adjective-spoiled, adverb-quickly.*

3. Select one series of words that are the same part of speech, and add this parallel list to a sentence in your essay. Rewrite the sentence as needed to express a clear, complete thought: *Edmund should heed, follow, and obey the White Witch.*

Examples

From J. R. R. Tolkien's *The Hobbit*

"Not a *nasty, dirty, wet* hole, filled with the ends of worms and an oozy smell . . ."

From J. R. R. Tolkien's *The Hobbit*

". . . nor yet a *dry, bare, sandy* hole with nothing in it to sit down on or to eat: it was a hobbit hole, and that means comfort."

From Earnest Hemingway's *A Farewell to Arms*

"What a beautiful bridge," Aymo said. It was a *long plain iron* bridge across what was usually a dry river-bed."

EXAMPLE

Term
Edmund

Nouns
Lucy, Susan, Peter

Parallel Structure
Edmund, Lucy, Susan, and Peter are siblings.

Verb
Heed, follow, obey

Parallel Structure
Edmund should heed, follow, and obey the White Witch.

Adjectives
Spoiled, angry, jealous

Parallel Structure
The spoiled, jealous, angry Edmund considered the White Witch's offer.

Adverb
Quickly, willingly, foolishly

Parallel Structure
Edmund followed the Witch quickly, willingly, and foolishly.

Practice

1. List two terms from your issue.

_____

_____

Move these terms to the chart below.

2. List parts of speech for each term using the corresponding boxes in the chart.

PART OF SPEECH	TERM A_____	TERM B_____
Nouns (list nouns related to your term):		
Verbs (list actions related to your term):		
Adjectives (list adjectives related to the term):		
Adverbs (list adverbs related to a verb or adjective above):		

3. Use two or three words from one list to create sentences with parallel word structure. Be sure to check your sentence construction. Parallel lists need proper punctuation and conjunctions.

_____

_____

TIPS

<u>Pairs</u> will be joined with a conjunction.

A <u>series</u> is a group of three or more elements in a row.
The last element in the series is usually connected to the others
with one of these coordinating conjunctions: *and, or, but (not), or
yet (not).*

<u>Commas</u> should be placed between each element in the series and before the
coordinating conjunction.

Now add your own examples of parallelism to Essay Two.

ESSAY THREE

Essay Three Invention
COMPARISON I: SIMILARITIES

Tools For The Teacher

Essay Three Invention Worksheet (page 23 in the Student Workbook)
Samples from this lesson guide for class discussion

Definition

- ❖ **Comparison**
  One of the Five Common Topics of Invention, Comparison asks how two terms (things, characters, places, ideas, etc.) are similar by noting what both terms "have," "are," and "do."

Background for the Teacher

- ❖ **Idea:** By discovering similarities between terms, students gather information about their issues and add it to their ANI charts or Invention worksheets. They are learning to think closely and more deeply.

- ❖ Students learn that they can generate information about an Issue and its terms by using the Topic of Comparison.

- ❖ Remember that the Invention lessons always start a new essay, and the skills from previous lesson are repeated for each new essay. Students begin a new essay by forming a new Issue and starting a new ANI.

Your Students Will Learn How to:

- ✓ Use the Topic of Comparison to discover similarities between terms
- ✓ Add the information generated to their ANI charts and use it to think about their Issue

Steps to Teach This Lesson

☐ **Select two physical things to compare,** such as an apple and orange, a pen and pencil, or a car and truck, and ask students to describe ways the two objects are similar.

For this first comparison, choose two concrete items that your students can see. Discovering similarities among physical objects prepares them to compare characters and places from books and stories.

☐ **Show** your students how to compare any two objects by finishing the following phrases:

- Both **are** . . .
- Both **have** . . .
- Both **do** . . .

> ***Teaching Tip***
>
> When deciding what two things, characters, places, or ideas to compare there is no such thing as "too random". In fact, it can prove quite useful to compare, for example, characters from different books, a literary character with a historic character, or even a character with a piece of fruit. You just never know what a student will discover!

Note: The Topic of Comparison is amazingly powerful. The questions above help us learn about the things our terms name and thus make better decisions. By practicing these generative questions, your students are gaining a potent new tool to use when they write, think, communicate, and make decisions.

☐ Next, **compare two characters from your issue or a character from your issue with another character in the story**, such as Edmund and the White Witch from *The Lion, the Witch, and the Wardrobe*. Be sure to use the "are, have, and do" questions you taught previously. Here is a very brief example of the process. Your comparison lesson will likely generate a much greater wealth of information.

- ❖ **Issue:** *Whether Edmund should have followed the White Witch*
- ❖ **Terms to compare:** Edmund, the White Witch
- ❖ **Both are:** In Narnia, cold, manipulative, cunning, bossy, sneaky
- ❖ **Both have:** Hair, homes, been to London
- ❖ **Both do:** Want something, talk, know the Beavers, want to be in charge, act mean, talk to animals

☐ As your students generate information, **create a list of similarities** between the two terms. All of this information should be considered part of the I column in the ANI chart.

☐ After the list **of similarities** is created, review it to see if any information or ideas can be used to support the affirmative or negative case. Move any appropriate material to the corresponding column in the ANI chart.

☐ Model the comparison process several times using various examples. As always, particularly in the Canon of Invention, **allow time for thinking, make generous use of the topic questions, and give students the freedom to generate ideas**. It is not time yet to be driven by the need to complete the essay or to worry about words, but to enjoy the time of contemplation.

☐ **Review** by asking students how they used the Topic of Comparison to generate information and where they put it. Encourage them to explain Comparison (and the steps you went through for each example) in their own words. Ask them questions like the following:

- *What did we do today to gather more invention material?*
- *What questions did we ask to find these similarities?*
- *How did we use this information on the ANI chart?*
- *How will you use this to complete your next Invention assignment?*
- *If you feel brave you could even ask: How will you use this to make better decisions?*

☐ **Assign** Essay Three Student Worksheet (page 23 in the Student Workbook), for their essays.

Examples

Example A
from The Lion, the Witch, and the Wardrobe *by C.S. Lewis*

❖ **Issue:** *Whether Edmund should have followed the White Witch*

❖ **Terms to compare:** Edmund, the White Witch

❖ **Both are:** In Narnia, cold, manipulative, cunning, bossy, sneaky

❖ **Both have:** Hair, homes, been to London

- ❖ **Both do:** Want something, talk, know the Beavers, want to be in charge, act mean, talk to animals

---

Example B
from "The Gift of the Magi" by O Henry

- ❖ **Issue:** *Whether Della should cut her hair*
- ❖ **Terms to compare:** Della, Mrs. Santa Claus
- ❖ **Both are:** Married, emotional
- ❖ **Both have:** Homes, responsibility
- ❖ **Both do:** Wear clothes, love their husbands

Example C
from The Odyssey *by Homer*

- ❖ **Issue:** *Whether Odysseus should listen to the Sirens*
- ❖ **Terms to comapare:** Odysseus' crew, the Sirens
- ❖ **Both are:** Living creatures, with Odysseus, far from Ithaka, working
- ❖ **Both have:** Desires, resources, companions, voices
- ❖ **Both do:** Talk/call to Odysseus, try to get what they want, act, sing

Assessment
Confirm that students:

- ✓ Understand how to compare two terms using have, are, and do

- ✓ Have generated enough similarities and added them to their ANI chart or worksheets

- ✓ Have moved any relevant points from the Comparison worksheet to their A and N columns

SAMPLE STUDENT WORKSHEET

Essay Three Invention
COMPARISON I: SIMILARITIES

List the two terms you will compare.

A_____   B_____

WHAT DO BOTH HAVE?	WHAT ARE BOTH?	WHAT DO BOTH DO?

Review your I column and move any appropriate items to the A or N columns.

Essay Three Arrangement
EXORDIUM

Tools for the Teacher

Essay Three Arrangement Worksheets (page 24 in the Student Workbook)
Essay Three Arrangement Template (page 28 in the Student Workbook)
Samples from this lesson guide for class discussion

Definitions

- **Exordium**
  The opening of an essay or speech, placed at the beginning of the Introduction. Its purpose is to make the audience members receptive to the speech or essay so they will listen.

Background for the Teacher

- **Idea:** Students will learn that the exordium is the opening to an essay, placed at the beginning of the Introduction.

- Students will learn and practice **three** ways to open an essay: asking questions, challenging the audience, and quoting an apt source.

- The plural of Exordium is "Exordia."

Note: This lesson introduces an idea that students will refine as long as they write or communicate. In previous lessons they have learned about the Proof, the part of the essay that is most logical or rational. The Exordium is much more psychological, so its uses are more subtle and complex. Indeed, because it becomes so complex, it is important to keep it simple for Level 1. Even so, the Exordium exercises will make them more aware of and attentive to their audience.

In addition, as your students grow in their understanding of rhetoric, they will discover many more ways to open an essay. Remember that they have plenty of room to grow in the art of persuasion.

Your Students Will Learn:

- ✓ What an Exordium is
- ✓ Three kinds of Exordium
- ✓ How to generate each kind of Exordium and add them to the Outline
- ✓ Where the Exordium belongs in the outline

Steps to Teach This Lesson

☐ **Discuss** with your students how beginnings are different from the other parts of events, artifacts, and even natural objects.

Here are some questions to get you started.

- *"When you read the first few sentences of a written story or article, how do you decide whether to continue? Do things change after the beginning?"*

- *"How do movies usually open? Do they stay the same throughout the movie?"*

- *"Do compositions have an opening? What is a musical introduction and what purpose does it serve?"*

☐ **Model** the different kinds of Exordium with your class. You can find several examples below, and you should add examples from your class work. Together generate examples of questions, quotations, and challenges that they might be able to use in their own essays.

> **Teaching Tip**
>
> As you teach the Exordium, remember that students should already have an Issue, sorted ANI, thesis, and proofs for this lesson. Do not try to teach them the Exordium disconnected from the thesis and proofs, as they are learning that the Exordium draws the reader in and points them to their thesis.

For each example, present these steps:

- ○ *List the Thesis.*
- ○ *List the 3 Proofs.*
- ○ *Generate at least one Exordium of each type to fit your Thesis and Proofs.*
- ○ *Select one Exordium for your essay.*

Since the Exordium opens the essay, it will be the **first point** on their outline. However, it must not be created until after the Proof. Remind them that the Order of Development (the Exordium is *developed* last) must be different from the Order of Presentation (the Exordium is *presented* first).

☐ After students have practiced with your guidance, **Review,** with several guiding questions, the kinds, place, and use of the Exordium.

- *How did you develop your first Exordium?*
- *Where did it go?*
- *How else did you generate Exordia?*
- *Where did they go?*
- *When do you develop the Exordia?*

☐ **Assign** *Essay Three Worksheet: A Guide to Exordium* (page 24 in the Students Workbook) for students to complete with their Essay Three Issue.

☐ **Assign** Essay Three Arrangement Worksheet (page 25 in the workbook) and Essay Three Template (page 28 in the workbook).

☐ Students will list the Thesis, Proofs, and Conclusion before the Exordium and the rest of Introduction. Students must establish the argument before deciding how to open an essay.

Examples

Example A
from The Lion, the Witch, and the Wardrobe

- ❖ **Thesis:** *Edmund should not have followed the White Witch*

- ❖ **Ask 3 Questions**

    - Can you imagine what it would be like to work with a Queen?
    - Have you ever met a member of royalty?
    - What would you do if a pale, white, icy lady asked you to follow her?

- ❖ **List two things you can <u>challenge</u> your readers to do that will arouse their attention.** *These should be written as imperative statements.*
    - Try to say "no" to someone you are afraid of!

- Dare to turn down a Queen who demands your allegiance!

❖ **Provide a <u>quotation</u> relevant to the issue**

"A strength to harm is perilous in the hand of an ambitious head."
-Queen Elizabeth I

❖ **Outline Template Sample** (the added element in bold)

I. Introduction
    A. Exordium
    B. Thesis: Edmund should not have followed the White Witch.
    C. Enumeration: 3 reasons
    D. Exposition
        1. ignored a warning
        2. overlooked the evil
        3. acted in secret

Example B
from "The Gift of the Magi"

❖ **Thesis:** *Della should cut her hair*

❖ **Ask 3 <u>Questions</u>**

- How much would you sacrifice for someone you love?
- What is the most extravagant gift you have ever received?
- Is the value of a gift the value of love?

❖ **List two things you can <u>challenge</u> your readers to do that will arouse their attention.** *These should be written as imperative statements.*

- Imagine giving up your most precious possession.
- Consider putting a dollar amount on one of your body parts.

❖ **Provide a <u>quotation</u> relevant to the issue**

- *Source:* Proverbs 15:17
  Quotation: "Better is a dinner of herbs where love is than a fatted calf with hatred."

❖ **Outline Template Sample** (the added element in bold)

    I. Introduction
        A. Exordium
        B. Thesis: Della should cut her hair.
        C. Enumeration: 3 reasons
        D. Exposition
            1. Sacrifice
            2. Love
            3. Christmas

Assessment
Confirm that students have:

    ✓ Completed the Exordium Worksheet for their current essay

    ✓ Completed the Essay Three Arrangement Worksheet

    ✓ Imitated the Arrangement Three Template for their current essay

SAMPLE STUDENT WORKSHEET

Essay Three Arrangement A
A GUIDE TO EXORDIUM

Use each of the following kinds of Exordium to generate possible openings for your essay.

Ask three questions.

_____
_____
_____

Write two things you can challenge your readers to do.

_____
_____

Provide a quotation relevant to the issue.

Source:

_____
_____

Quotation:

_____
_____
_____
_____
_____

Essay Three Arrangement Template
BASIC PERSUASIVE ESSAY

Transcribe your outline onto a separate page, imitating the template provided below. Do not use complete sentences.

Replace lines that have an asterisk with *your* information from the Arrangement Worksheet on the previous pages.

I. Introduction

    A. *Exordium* *
    B. *Thesis* *
    C. *Enumeration* *
    D. *Exposition*
        1. Proof I*
        2. Proof II*
        3. Proof III*

II. Proof

    A. *Proof I* *
        1. Sub-Proof 1*
        2. Sub-Proof 2*
        3. Sub-Proof 3*
    B. *Proof II* *
        1. Sub-Proof 1*
        2. Sub-Proof 2*
        3. Sub-Proof 3*
    C. *Proof III* *
        1. Sub-Proof 1*
        2. Sub-Proof 2*
        3. Sub-Proof 3*

III. Conclusion

    A. *Thesis* *

    B. *Summary of Proof*
        1. Proof I*
        2. Proof II*
        3. Proof III*

Essay Three Elocution
VERBS

Tools for the Teacher

Essay Three Elocution Worksheet (page 29 in the Student Workbook)
Samples from this lesson guide for class discussion

Background for the Teacher

- ❖ **Idea:** Active and precise verbs make writing clearer and livelier.

- ❖ Using vivid verbs is a skill of both composition (i.e. choosing the right word at the right time) and editing (i.e. learning to spot the wrong word and correct it). Your goal is to cultivate perception and judgment through practice. Practice and gentle coaching will nurture judgment and help your students see that most "rules" are generally reliable but should not be slavishly followed.

  Worksheets are a valuable tool for introducing and practicing the concept, but the real growth happens when students begin to correct errors in their own writing.

Your Students Will Learn:

- ✓ To pay closer attention to the verbs they use
- ✓ To replace vague and passive verbs with precise and active verbs

Steps to Teach This Lesson

☐ To begin, discuss verbs. It can also be helpful to talk about how we are constantly self-editing. Here are some sample questions to get you started.

- *What is a verb?*
- *List several verbs.*

- *Which are active?*
- *Which are passive?*
- *Which are vague and which precise? (This is a difference in degree, so answers might vary.)*
- *Have you ever started to say something, hesitated, and started over?*
- *What would cause that?*
- *What good would come of starting over?*
- *Would that apply to writing as well?*

☐ Help students build stronger sentences with two kinds of verbs:

- Precise verbs
- Active verbs

Step #1 – Use Precise Verbs

Conversational patterns are often wordy and imprecise when used in writing. Present the following sentences:

1. He got a gift from Father Christmas.
2. She got a glimpse of the faun.
3. They had a chance to sail home.
4. He has shiny armor.
5. The wolf went out in search of the children and beavers.
6. The teenagers went for a walk through the new house.

Rewrite each sentence above, replacing each vague verb (have/had/has, go/went, and get/got) with a more precise verb. Explain how they "got," "had," or "went."

Step #2 – Use Active Verbs

Verbs can be active or passive in voice, but too many passive verbs make writing sleepy. When the subject of the sentence does the acting, the verb is active. When the subject is acted on, the verb is passive.

Present the following sentences, noting the passive verbs. Ask your students to find the actor in each:

1. The sleigh is being driven fast.
2. Mrs. Jones' floor is being cleaned by her daughter.
3. In the tent, the armor was left abandoned by Achilles.
4. During Narnian winter, the fauns were turned to stone by the White Witch.
5. The wardrobe was entered separately.
6. The wine-dark sea was navigated skillfully.

Sometimes actors are hidden in the back of the sentence by passive verbs. Sometimes they are removed completely. Writers who desire to craft strong sentences use passive verbs only when necessary.

Show your students how to change the verbs from passive voice to active.

- First, make the actor the subject. Either find it in the sentence or create one. (e.g. "The dwarf")

- Second, make the verb active so it goes with the new subject (e.g. drives or is driving).

- Third, complete the sentence (e.g. The dwarf is driving the sleigh fast).

☐ **Review** the steps you took when you edited verbs.

- *When checking for imprecise verbs, what verbs did you look for?*
- *How did you rewrite the sentences?*
- *When checking for passive verbs, what did you look for?*
- *How did you rewrite those sentences?*
- *Can you think of any more imprecise verbs to beware of? (Note: "Are", "have", and "do" are great Invention verbs because they are so general, but they are usually poor Elocution verbs for the same reason!)*
- *What will you do to avoid vague and passive verbs in your writing?*

☐ **Assign** Essay Three Elocution Worksheet (page 29 in the Student Workbook) unless you completed this work together in class.

☐ Students will check the verbs in their essays. Note that each Proof sentence is likely to use the "be" verb (The first reason is...). This is not passive in voice and is a legitimate use of the "be" verb.

☐ **Remind** students to check their essays against the Essay Three checklist

---

Examples

- From Herman Melville's *Moby Dick*

    *"Such a portentous and mysterious monster **roused** all my curiosity."*

- From Genesis 2:7

    *"And the LORD God **formed** man of the dust of the ground, and **breathed** into his nostrils the breath of life; and man became a living soul."*

- From John Magee's "High Flight"

    *"Oh! I have **slipped** the surly bonds of Earth
    And **danced** the skies on laughter-silvered wings ..."*

Assessment
Confirm that students have:

- ✓ Completed the Essay Three Elocution: Verbs Worksheet
- ✓ Checked the current essay for vague and passive verbs, replacing as necessary
- ✓ Written Essay Three, referring to the Essay Three checklist for self-editing

<u>Tip</u>

*As you review the current essay, pay special attention
to the kinds of verbs used. If the student uses the occasional "to be"
or passive verb, that's fine. If you see a preponderance of imprecise or passive
verbs, ask for revisions. Look for and commend particularly strong verbs.*

SAMPLE STUDENT WORKSHEET

Essay Three Elocution
BASIC EDITING: VERBS

What is a verb?

_____

_____

Examples of Active and Precise Verbs

❖ From Herman Melville's *Moby Dick*

"Such a portentous and mysterious monster **roused** all my curiosity."

❖ From Genesis 2:7

"And the LORD God **formed** man of the dust of the ground, and **breathed** into his nostrils the breath of life; and man became a living soul."

❖ From John Magee's "High Flight"

"Oh! I have **slipped** the surly bonds of Earth
And **danced** the skies on laughter-silvered wings ..."

Building Stronger Sentences

Step #1: Use Precise Verbs

Conversational patterns are often wordy and imprecise when used in writing. Consider the following sentences:

1. *He got a gift from Father Christmas.*

2. She got a glimpse of the faun.
3. They had a chance to sail home.
4. He has shiny armor.
5. The wolf went out in search of the children and beavers.
6. The children went for a walk through the new house.

Rewrite each sentence above, replacing each *have/had/has*, *go/went*, and *get/got* with an action verb. Communicate the action with more precision.

1. _____
2. _____
3. _____
4. _____
5. _____
6. _____

Step #2: Use Active Verbs

A passive verb hides the actor of a sentence.

Consider the following sentences:
1. The sleigh was being driven fast.
2. Mrs. Jones' floor was cleaned by her daughter.
3. In the tent, the armor was left abandoned by Achilles.
4. During Narnian winter, the fauns were turned to stone by the White Witch.
5. The wardrobe was entered separately.
6. The wine-dark sea was navigated skillfully.

Rewrite each sentence above with a more active verb.

1. _____
2. _____
3. _____

4. _____

5. _____

6. _____

Practice

Generate your own sentences:

1. List three subjects.

_____

_____

_____

2. With those subjects, write sentences with precise, active verbs.

_____

_____

_____

_____

_____

Essay Application

Check your current essay for vague and passive verbs.
Correct those sentences as necessary.

ESSAY FOUR

Essay Four Invention

COMPARISON II: DEGREE & KIND

Tools for The Teacher

Essay Four Invention Worksheet (page 35 in the Student Workbook)
Samples from this lesson guide for class discussion
Comparison One work from the previous lesson

Definitions

- **Differences of Degree**
  Differences of Degree are expressed when **one term is, has, or does more or less than other term**. This is commonly expressed with the words more/less and better/worse.

- **Differences of Kind**
  Differences of Kind are expressed when one term **belongs to a different group** than another term.

Background for the Teacher

- **Idea:** Students learn to examine the differences between terms by identifying two kinds of difference: differences of degree and differences of kind.

- Remember that the Invention lessons always start a new essay, and the skills from previous lesson are repeated for each new essay. Students begin a new essay by forming a new issue and starting a new ANI.

Your Students Will Learn How to:

✓ Ask questions about difference of degree (more/less and better/worse)
✓ Ask questions about difference of kind (what kind of thing is the term?)
✓ Add information generated to their ANI charts

Steps to Teach Differences of Degree and Kind

☐ Review the previous Invention lesson, Comparison One. Ask students how they found the similarities between two terms. They should be able to model this with these phrases:

- Both **are** . . .
- Both **have** . . .
- Both **do** . . .

☐ **As with Comparison One, start by introducing this idea with physical objects,** such as an apple and orange. Introducing the ideas with physical, easy-to-see objects eases the transition to comparing literary and historical characters and places.

☐ Next, guide them to think about **differences of degree**. Ask whether Term A or B is more/less or better/worse. The worksheet provides a box for each difference in degree with the "more/less" and "better/worse" categories.

Here are some samples:

o **Are:** *An apple is less juicy than an orange, an apple is less flavorful than an orange, an apple is more firm than the orange.*

o **Have:** *An apple's skin is less thick than the orange's, an apple is less full of seeds than the orange.*

o **Does:** *An apple rots more (faster) than an orange, an apple satisfies me more than an orange.*

Do not feel compelled to find a difference of degree for every similarity listed. Keep this lesson generative and encourage students to keep thinking.

☐ Next, **move on to Differences of Kind.** Start by identifying the groups that both terms belong to (i.e., apples and oranges are both foods, fruits, snacks, and carbohydrates). Then identify the differences of kind:

> o *While an apple is a pomme fruit, an orange is a citrus fruit.*
>
> o *While an apple is a fruit with an edible skin, an orange is a fruit with an inedible skin.*

☐ Now **practice** this process with character terms, like Edmund and the White Witch, repeating this process with several additional examples.

☐ After the Comparison of Degree and Kind is created, **go back over the list of similarities and differences to see if anything can be used to support the affirmative or negative sides of your issue**.

☐ **Review** by asking students several questions. Encourage students to explain Comparison (and the steps you went through for each example) in their own words. Ask them questions like the following:

- *What did we do today to gather more Invention material?*
- *What questions did we ask to find these differences?*
- *What kinds of differences did we use?*
- *How did we use this information on the ANI chart?*
- *How will you apply differences to your Invention?*

☐ **Assign** Essay Four Invention Worksheet: Comparison Two (page 35 in the Student Workbook) for their own essays

---

Examples

> **Example A**
> *from* The Lion, the Witch, and the Wardrobe

- ❖ **Issue:** *Whether Edmund should have follow the White Witch*

- ❖ **Terms to compare:** *Edmund, the White Witch*

- ❖ **Both are:** *In Narnia, cold, manipulative, cunning, bossy, sneaky*

- ❖ **Both have:** *Hair, homes, been to London*

- ❖ **Both do:** *Want something, talk, know the Beavers, want to be in charge, act mean, talk to animals*

- ❖ **Differences of Degree:**

    - Does: *Edmund wants less power than the White Witch, the White Witch wears a warmer coat than Edmund*

    - Has: *The White Witch has better hair than Edmund, Edmund has traveled less than the White Witch, the White Witch has more acquaintances than Edmund*

    - Are: *Edmund is colder than the White Witch, the White Witch is more manipulative than Edmund*

- ❖ **Differences of Kind:**

    - Common groups: *Both Edmund and the White Witch are creatures, seekers, characters in the Narnia series, and creations of C.S. Lewis*
    -
    - Differences: *While Edmund is a human boy, the White Witch is a native of Charn*

Example B
from "The Gift of the Magi"

- ❖ **Issue:** *Whether Della should cut her hair*

- ❖ **Terms to compare?** *Della, Jane Eyre*

- ❖ **Both are:** *young, poor*

- ❖ **Both have:** *hair, husbands, determination*

- ❖ **Both do:** *dwell, work, want*

- ❖ **Differences of Degree:**

    - Does: *Della wants more elaborate things than Jane Eyre, Della dwells in a smaller home than Jane Eyre*

- Has: *Della has better hair than Jane Eyre, Della has a younger husband than Jane Eyre*

- Are: *At one point, Della is less poor than Jane Eyre*

❖ **Differences of Kind:**

- Common Groups: *Both Della and Jane Eyre are women, workers, and characters in a story.*

- Differences: *While Della is a married woman for the whole story, Jane is single for much of her story; while Della is a house worker, Jane is a music teacher.*

Example C
from "Androcles and the Lion"

❖ **Issue:** *Whether Androcles should have been punished*

❖ **Terms to compare?** *Androcles, the lion*

❖ **Both are:** *Compassionate, fleeing, needy, brave*

❖ **Both have:** *Flaws, troubles, masters*

❖ **Both do:** *Travel, hide, help befriend*

❖ **Differences of Degree:**

- Does: *Androcles travels more than the lion, running from his master and wandering in the woods; the lion helps more than Androcles by feeding, sheltering, and saving him.*

- Has: *Androcles has more fear than the lion: fearing the lion, his master, and the Emperor.*

- Are: *Androcles is more needy than the lion as he needs protection, food, and shelter*

❖ **Differences of Kind:**

- Common Groups: *living beings, Roman, outcasts, characters*

- Differences: *While Androcles is a man, the lion is an animal.*

Assessment
Confirm that students:

- ✓ Understand what Differences of Degree are and what Differences of Kind are

- ✓ Have offered enough points of Comparison

- ✓ Have moved any relevant points from the Comparison worksheets to their ANI charts

SAMPLE STUDENT WORKSHEET

Essay Four Invention
COMPARISON II: DIFFERENCES

List the two terms you will compare.

A_____ B_____

BOTH A & B DO (LIST VERBS):	A does more/less _____ *Verb* than B (describe the difference).	A does _____ *Verb* better/worse than B (describe the difference).
BOTH A & B HAVE (LIST NOUNS BOTH HAVE):	A has more/less _____ *Noun* than B (describe the difference).	A has better/worse _____ *Noun* than B (describe the difference).
BOTH A & B ARE (LIST ADJECTIVES BOTH SHARE)	A is more _____ *Adjective* than B (describe the difference).	
BOTH A & B ARE (LIST GROUPS BOTH BELONG TO)		A is better/worse _____ *Group Member* than B (describe the difference):

Identify one different group to which each term belongs and use those groups to complete the following sentence.

Examples:

While Edmund is a human boy, the White Witch is a native of Charn. While an apple is a pomme fruit, an orange is a citrus fruit.

While Achilles is a Greek, Hector is a Trojan.

While_____(Term A) is

_____(a group or kind of thing),

_____(Term B) is

_____(a different group or kind of thing).

Review your I column, and move any appropriate items to the A or N columns.

Essay Four Arrangement
AMPLIFICATION

Tools for the Teacher

Essay Four Arrangement Worksheets (page 37 in the Student Workbook)
Student work from Invention Four
Samples from this lesson guide for class discussion

Definitions

- **Amplification**
  Part of the essay's conclusion in which the writer states to whom his Issue matters and why it matters to that person or group.

Background for the Teacher

- **Idea:**. The Amplification is an additional statement directly following the restatement of the Thesis and Proofs in the conclusion that answers the questions, "who cares?" and "why?"

Your Students Will Learn to:

- ✓ Identify their audience
- ✓ Select groups this audience cares about
- ✓ Show how the Issue will affect this group
- ✓ Write an Amplification to explain why this audience should care about their Thesis

Steps to Teach This Lesson

☐ **Discuss how lawyers end their arguments or speakers end their persuasive speeches**. You might read an example of a famous closing argument or even play a clip. Either way, help students see that we end an argument with a summary of the argument and statement of why this position matters. This idea prepares students to think about improving their persuasive essay conclusion. Here are a few examples:

From Atticus Finch's closing argument in To Kill a Mockingbird:

"Now, gentlemen, in this country our courts are the great levelers. In our courts, all men are created equal. I'm no idealist to believe firmly in the integrity of our courts and of our jury system. That's no ideal to me. That is a living, working reality! Now I am confident that you gentlemen will review without passion the evidence that you have heard, come to a decision, and restore this man to his family. In the name of God, do your duty. In the name of God, believe Tom Robinson."

From Ad Herennium, 4.40.52:

"He [the defendant] is the betrayer of his own self-respect, and the waylayer of the self-respect of others; covetous, intemperate, irascible, arrogant; disloyal to his parents, ungrateful to his friends, troublesome to his kin; insulting to his betters, disdainful of his equals and mates, cruel to his inferiors; in short, he is intolerable to everyone."

From Martin Luther King Junior's "I Have a Dream" Speech:

And when this happens, when we allow freedom to ring, when we let it ring from every village and every hamlet, from every state and every city, we will be able to speed up that day when *all* of God's children, black men and white men, Jews and Gentiles, Protestants and Catholics, will be able to join hands and sing in the words of the old Negro spiritual: *Free at last! Free at last! Thank God Almighty, we are free at last!*

☐ **Model and practice several examples** of creating Amplification. We have included several examples for you below. Use issues with which your students are particularly familiar as well.

<u>Steps to creating an Amplification</u>

    1. State the Thesis

    2. Identify the audience (list several options and select one)

- Option 1 - The actor in the Issue: *Edmund*

- Option 2 - Another group who can judge the decision: *My teacher, my friends, the Narnians, Lucy*

3. Select a group or person the audience cares about (The student worksheet provides many categories to choose from.)

- Edmund: *siblings, Narnia*
- My friends: *each other, their siblings, God, their parents*

4. Explain why the audience cares (i.e. how does this Issue affect this group or person?)

- *This decision caused trouble for Edmund's siblings and Narnia.*

5. Express this idea as an Amplification (Students often need to practice stating the Thesis together with the Amplification to verify that it logically follows.)

- *Edmund caused tremendous trouble not only for himself, but— even worse—for his siblings and for all of Narnia.*

☐ **Show your students where the Amplification belongs**, both in the order of development on the Worksheet and in the Template.

☐ Ask the students to **compare and review** the various Amplifications they completed. *What steps did they take to create each one? What two groups did you need to identify each time? Where does the Amplification go in the outline?*

☐ **Assign** Essay Four Arrangement Amplification Worksheet (page 37 in the Student Workbook), for their own essays. Then they will complete the Essay Four Arrangement Worksheet (page 39) and Essay Four Arrangement Template (page 42 in the Workbook).

Examples

Example A
from "The Gift of the Magi"

- ❖ **Thesis:** *Della should cut her hair.*

- ❖ **Identify the audience** (list several options and select one)
  - Della
  - The community, my teacher, Della's husband, girls in my class, my friends

- ❖ **Select groups or a person this audience cares about**
  (The student worksheet provides many categories to choose from.)
  My friends: their family, their friends, women everywhere

- ❖ **Explain why the audience cares (i.e. how does this issue affect this group or person?)** My friends will see an example of sacrificing to give gifts.

- ❖ **Express this idea as an Amplification**: *Della should sell her hair because she can sacrifice, show love, and celebrate Christmas. This matters to our friends as we all need a picture of what Christmas is truly about. What matters is not the value of the gifts one receives, but of the gifts one gives.*

Example B
from Rikki Tikki Tavi

- ❖ **Thesis:** *Teddy should have kept Rikki Tikki Tavi for a pet.*

- ❖ **Identify the audience** (list several options and select one)
  - Teddy
  - Teddy's family, the animals in the garden, other people in India

- ❖ **Select group or person this audience cares about**
  (The student worksheet provides many categories to choose from.)

> Teddy's family: the children, visitors, themselves

- ❖ **Explain why the audience cares (ie how does this issue affect this group or person?)** They need and want a safe, happy home

- ❖ **Express this idea as an Amplification:** *Teddy should have kept Rikki for a pet because Rikki was protective, he was a good pet for Teddy, and he himself needed a good home.* ***Thanks to the attentiveness of Rikki Tikki Tavi, Teddy and his family had a safer and thus happier home.***

Assessment
Confirm that students have:

- ✓ Completed the Amplification worksheet for Essay Four
- ✓ Completed the Essay Four Arrangement worksheet
- ✓ Transcribed the Arrangement Four Template for their current essay

<u>*Tip:*</u>

Remember quality increases with maturity, practice, and exposure to great literature, so be patient!

SAMPLE STUDENT WORKSHEET

Essay Four Arrangement A

BASIC PERSUASIVE ESSAY WITH AMPLIFICATION

Write your Thesis statement.
_____

Identify your audience.
_____

Select the person or groups the audience cares about, and explain how the group will be affected by this issue.

- o Animals or an animal
   _____

- o Family or family members
   _____

- o Friends of your audience
   _____

- o Ancestors
   _____

- o Descendants
   _____

- o A specific group of people (identify)
   _____

- o Local community
   _____

- Community leaders

  _____

- Government (local, state, national)

  _____

- Voluntary Organizations (e.g. Church, Boy Scouts)

  _____

- God

  _____

- Other

  _____

Choose the one thing, person, or group on whom your Thesis would have the most impact.

- To whom your Thesis matters

  _____

- Why does your Thesis matter to them?

  _____

Essay Four Arrangement Template
BASIC PERSUASIVE ESSAY

Transcribe your outline onto a separate page, using the template provided below. Do not use complete sentences.

Replace lines that have an asterisk with *your* information from the Arrangement Worksheet on the previous pages.

I. Introduction
    A. Exordium*
    B. Thesis*
    C. Enumeration*
    D. Exposition*
        1. Proof I*
        2. Proof II*
        3. Proof III*

II. Proof
    A. Proof I*
        1. Sub-Proof 1*
        2. Sub-Proof 2*
        3. Sub-Proof 3*
    B. Proof II*
        1. Sub-Proof 1*
        2. Sub-Proof 2*
        3. Sub-Proof 3*
    C. Proof III*
        1. Sub-Proof 1*
        2. Sub-Proof 2*
        3. Sub-Proof 3*

III. Conclusion
    A. Thesis*
    B. Summary of Proof
        1. Proof I*
        2. Proof II*
        3. Proof III*
    C. Amplification
        1. To whom it matters*
        2. Why it matters to that person or group*

Essay Four Elocution
PARALLELISM II

Tools for the Teacher

Essay Four Elocution Worksheet (page 43 in the Student Workbook)
Samples from this lesson guide for class discussion

Definitions

❖ **Parallelism:** A similarity of structure in a pair or series of related words, phrases, or clauses (sentences).

Background for the Teacher

❖ **Idea:** Parallelism is similarity of structure in a pair or series of related words, phrases, or clauses and gives harmonious form, interest, and beauty to a sentence or passage.

As they master parallel structure, your students will come to use many other types of parallelism, as well.

Your Students Will Learn to:

✓ Write sentences using parallel phrases and clauses

Steps to Teach This Lesson

☐ **Review** Parallelism 1, writing with parallel series of words. Ask students to read their parallel sentences both from the worksheet and from their essays.

☐ Students will need to understand what a phrase and a clause are for this lesson. Take a few moments to **review** both ideas and clarify as needed.

> *Teaching Tip*
> This lesson builds on Parallelism 1, and students are now working with more complicated ideas. Your students will benefit from discussion and guidance from you, the teacher. You will be modeling the idea of Parallelism, practicing it, and gently correcting and encouraging them to take time to think about several options.

☐ **Present** several models of parallelism to your students. We have included several here and on the student worksheet. Remember that this lesson focuses on parallelism of phrases, clauses, and sentences.

☐ After reading and discussing the examples of parallelism, identifying the parallel type and structure in each, **show** your students how to apply it to their essays.

To expand your sentence by adding parallel phrases or clauses:

- Identify a sentence with a phrase or clause that contains a structure that can be imitated. Some possibilities: infinitives, noun phrases, adjective/adverb phrases or clauses, prepositional phrases (e.g. Prep: *In the beginning* she danced).
- Generate additional phrases or clauses that follow the same pattern as the one you chose above. e.g. *at the midpoint, over the top, around the end, after the conclusion*
- Select two phrases or clauses to add to the one you chose in the first step (e.g. *at the midpoint, after the conclusion*)
- Expand your sentence, adding the two new phrases or clauses and following the same pattern as the first. Make any other changes necessary to keep the sentence coherent. *In the beginning, at the midpoint, and after the conclusion, she never stopped dancing.*

To revise existing clauses or phrases (such as the Proofs):

- Choose a phrase or clause that follows a pattern that later phrases or clauses could imitate (for the sake of this exercise, treat a sentence like a clause). The first Proof can be very useful for this exercise because you know there will be a series of clauses that follows the same pattern.
  e.g. *Achilleus is fast.*
- Identify the pattern followed by your chosen phrase or clause.
  SN-V-Adj
- Find two other phrases or clauses that are related to the one you chose above.
- Compare their patterns to determine whether they can be made parallel to the first. Would their relationship to the first be clearer if they were made parallel?
- Try several different ways to make them parallel until you find the pattern that works best.
  e.g. *Achilleus is mighty.*
  e.g. *Achilleus is passionate.*

☐ **Review** how you created sentences with parallelism

- *What two ways can you add parallelism?*
- *What did you do first to expand your sentence with parallelism?*
- *What did you do next each time?*
- *How many phrases or clauses did you add to your sentence?*
- *What did you do first to revise the existing phrases or clauses?*
- *What pattern did you identify each time?*
- *What did you do to the next sentences to make them parallel?*

☐ **Assign** the *Essay Four Elocution: Parallelism 2* Worksheet (page 43 in the Workbook).

☐ Students will add one or more examples of parallelism to their essays.

Remind students to refer to the Essay Four checklist to confirm that they have completed their essays.

Examples

- From I Corinthins 13:11:

    When I was a child, I spoke as a child, I understood as a child, I thought as a child; but when I became a man, I put away childish things.

- From William Shakespeare's "Othello":

    I saw't not, thought it not, it harmed not me.

- From Dante's *Inferno*:

    "'Philosophy makes plain by many reasons,'
    he answered me, "to those who heed her teachings, how all of Nature,—her laws, her fruits, her seasons,— springs from the Ultimate Intellect and Its art..."

- From Washington Irving's "Rip Van Winkle":

    "Here they used to sit in the shade through a long lazy summer's day, talking listlessly over village gossip, or telling endless sleepy stories about nothing."

- From I Corinthians 13:4-7:

    Love suffers long and is kind; love does not envy; love does not parade itself, is not puffed up; does not behave rudely, does not seek its own, is not provoked, thinks no evil; does not rejoice in iniquity, but rejoices in the truth; bears all things, believes all things, hopes all things, endures all things.

Assessment
Confirm that students have:

- ✓ Completed *Essay Four Elocution: Parallelism Two* Worksheet
- ✓ Added parallelism to their current essay
- ✓ Written Essay Four, following the Essay Four checklist

SAMPLE STUDENT WORKSHEET

Essay Four Elocution
PARALLELISM II: PHRASES & CLAUSES

Definition

Parallelism is similarity of structure in a pair or series of related words, phrases, or clauses (sentences).

Review

1. List the parts of speech.
   _____

2. What is a phrase?
   _____

3. Give two examples of a phrase.
   _____
   _____

4. What is a clause?
   _____

5. Give two examples of clauses.
   _____
   _____

Examples

Words can be parallel, as in the following:

From Shakespeare's *The Tragedy of Julius Caesar*

"*Friends, Romans, Countrymen*, lend me your ears;
I come to bury Caesar, not to praise him."

From Washington Irving's "Rip Van Winkle"

"*Morning, noon, and night*, her tongue was incessantly going, and everything he said or did was sure to produce a torrent of household eloquence."

From Homer's *Iliad*

"...the shaker of the earth did not fail to hear the goddess, *but came* up among them from the sea, *and sat* in the midst of them, *and asked* Zeus of his counsel."
XX, 13-15

Phrases can be parallel, as in the following:

From the *Ad Herrenium*

"The Romans *destroyed Numantia, razed Carthage, obliterated Corinth, overthrew Fregellae*."

From Washington Irving's "Rip Van Winkle"

"Here they used to sit in the shade through a long lazy summer's day, *talking listlessly over village gossip, or telling endless sleepy stories about nothing.*"

Clauses can be parallel, as in the following:

From Plutarch's life of Julius Caesar

"I came; I saw; I conquered."

From Charles Dickens's *Great Expectations*

"A boy may lock his door, [he] may be warm in bed, [he] may tuck himself up, [he] may draw the clothes over his head, [he] may think himself comfortable, and safe, but that young man will softly creep and creep his way to him and tear him open."

Student Examples

The Nightingale should have returned to sing for the Emperor for three reasons: she brought him comfort, she saved him from Death, and she changed the Emperor to a better man.

Odysseus debated whether to pull out his sword, throw down his shield, and cut off his head.

> Socrates and Phaedrus should walk to the tall plane tree for three reasons: the walk will benefit their bodies, their minds, and their souls.

> Aeneas's identity demands his action, his action magnifies his reputation, and his reputation opens his future.

Steps to using parallelism in your sentence structure:

Either find a phrase or clause in your writing that you can expand by adding detail or use parallel structure to rewrite sentences you have already written. Your three Proofs are a great place to start.

If you want to add to a sentence:

a. Identify a sentence with a phrase or clause that contains a structure that can be imitated. Some things to look for: prepositional phrases, infinitives, noun phrases, or adjective/adverb clauses, e.g.. *"in the beginning"*.
b. Generate additional phrases or clauses that follow the same structure as the one you chose above, e.g., *"at the midpoint"*, *"after the end"*.
c. Select two phrases or clauses to add to the one you chose in step a.
d. Expand your sentence, adding the two new phrases or clauses and following the same pattern as the first. Make any other changes necessary to keep the sentence coherent.

If you want to rewrite existing clauses or phrases (such as your Proofs):

a. Choose a phrase or clause that follows a pattern that later phrases or clauses could imitate (for the sake of this exercise, treat a sentence like a clause). The first proof can be very useful for this exercise because you know there will be a series of clauses that follows the same pattern.
b. Identify the pattern followed by your chosen phrase or clause.
c. Find two other phrases or clauses that are related to the one you chose above.
d. Compare their patterns to determine whether they can be made parallel to the first. Would their relationship to the first be clearer if they were made parallel?
e. Try several different ways to make them parallel until you find the pattern that works best.

Practice

1. Add more details to a sentence.

    A. Pick a phrase or clause from your writing.

    _____

    _____

    B. Generate several additional phrases or clauses

    _____

    _____

2. Rewrite a sentence or several sentences with parallel structure.

    _____

    _____

    _____

TIPS

Remember to keep writing in parallel structure.
Keep an eye on those **parts of speech**!

Be sure to **check** your sentence construction.
Parallel **lists** need proper punctuation and conjunctions.

Pairs will be joined with a **conjunction.**

A **series** is a group of three or more elements in a row.
The last element in the series is commonly connected
to the others with one of these coordinating
conjunctions:
and, or, but (not), or yet (not).

Commas should be placed between each element in the series
and before the coordinating conjunction.

**Now add your own examples of
parallelism to Essay Four.**

ESSAY FIVE

Essay Five Invention
DEFINITION

Tools for the Teacher

Essay Five Invention Worksheet (page 51 in the Student Workbook)
Samples from this lesson guide for class discussion

Definitions

- **Term**
  Words or phrases used to name things

- **Genus**
  The category or group to which the thing defined belongs; the first part of a term's definition

- **Species**
  members of the group (genus) to which a term belongs

- **Differentiae**
  The differences between a term and the other members of its genus. In the Topic of Definition, we ask what group (genus) our term belongs to and how it is different from other members of the group.

Background for the Teacher

- **Idea:** Students define a term by identifying the group to which it belongs and how it differs from other members of that group.

  They use the Topic of Definition to elucidate their terms and to gather information for their ANI charts.

Terms can be defined many ways. Defining by genus and differentia (group and differences) is essential, but only one way. The goal of this lesson is not for students to copy the dictionary definition, but to generate their own definitions and thus to learn how definitions are developed and to better understand the ideas in their essays.

Students record the information gathered in the I column. At the end of the lesson, students review the I column and move any fitting ideas to the A and N columns.

❖ Remember that the Invention lessons always start a new essay, and the skills from previous lessons are repeated for each new essay. Students begin a new essay by forming a new issue and starting a new ANI.

Your Students Will Learn How to:

✓ Write their own definitions for terms by combining the group it belongs to (genus) with the unique characteristic of the term (differentia)

✓ Decide if anything they discover while defining their terms can be added to their A or N columns

Steps to Teach This Lesson

☐ **Discuss** how misunderstandings often occur when the parties involved define a word differently.

Start with some fun ways a term can be used in confusing ways:

- *My brother is always beating me. (Hopefully in a board or card game!)*
- *The mouse was under the table. (Preferably the computer mouse fell!)*

☐ **Complete** the steps of Definition together, as many times as needed.

When first you introduce the practice of Definition with your students, show them how to define nouns. Defining verbs can come later after they have had ample practice with defining nouns.

Begin with an item in the home/classroom that is very familiar and can be seen during this lesson.

- Pick a term to define.
- Identify several (3-4) groups that this term belongs to. (What kind of thing is this term?)
- Select the group that seems most helpful for this issue.
- List other members of the group you have selected.
- Identify a common characteristic of all members of this group. (What quality do all the members share?)
- List the unique characteristic of your term. (What makes your term different from the other members of this group?)
- Write your own definition for this term by combining the term, its group, and its unique characteristic.

☐ **Repeat** these steps to define multiple terms, using some of the examples below and terms from your own studies.

☐ **Review** the process of Definition by comparing the steps taken each time your students defined a term.

- *What step did you take first to define the first word?*
- *Did you do the same thing for the next word?*
- *What did you do next each time?*
  How did you decide which group to use?
- *Then what?*

☐ **Assign** the Essay Five Invention Worksheet (page 51 in the Workbook) using terms from their issues for Essay Five. You should decide how many terms you want your students to define based on readiness, need, and circumstances.

Examples

Example A
from The Lion, the Witch, and the Wardrobe

- ❖ **Issue:** *Whether Edmund should have follow the White Witch*
- ❖ **Term:** *Edmund*
- ❖ **Groups:** *Humans, boy characters in books, kings, brothers, nephews*
- ❖ **Choose a group:** *Boy characters in books*
- ❖ **Other members of the group:** *Tom Sawyer, Huck Finn, Jem Finch, Harry Potter*
- ❖ **Common characteristic:** *All go on adventures, all go on a journey of discovery, all are fictional*
- ❖ **Unique characteristic:** *In Chronicles of Narnia, from C.S. Lewis's imagination*

- ❖ **Definition:** *Edmund is a boy who is a fictional character in C.S. Lewis's Chronicles of Narnia books.*

Example B
from "The Gift of the Magi"

- ❖ **Issue:** *Whether Della should have cut her hair*
- ❖ **Term:** *Hair*
- ❖ **Groups:** *Accessories, non-living appendage, mammalian signifier, decorated body part*
- ❖ **Choose a group:** *Decorative body part*
- ❖ **Other members of the group:** *fingernails, toenails*
- ❖ **Common characteristic:** *Often trimmed or cut*
- ❖ **Unique characteristic:** *Regenerates itself very slowly*
- ❖ **Definition:** *Hair is a decorative body part that regenerates itself very slowly*

Example C
from The Odyssey

- ❖ **Issue:** *Whether Odysseus should have killed the suitors*
- ❖ **Term:** *Odysseus*
- ❖ **Groups:** *Husbands, fathers, rulers, warriors, wanderers*
- ❖ **Choose a group:** *Wanderers*
- ❖ **Other members of the group:** *Aeneas, John Coulter, Pilgrims, Goldilocks*
- ❖ **Common characteristic:** *People who are looking for a place to rest or call home*
- ❖ **Unique characteristic:** *Fought in the Trojan War, took ten years to return home, found home full of suitors courting his wife*
- ❖ **Definition:** *Odysseus was a wanderer who endured an adventurous ten-year journey from the Trojan War, where he fought. Upon returning home, he found his home full of suitors trying to court his wife.*

Example D

- ❖ **Term:** *George Washington*
- ❖ **Groups:** *Generals, Presidents, Gentlemen, land-owners*
- ❖ **Choose a group:** *Presidents*
- ❖ **Other members of the group:** *Thomas Jefferson, Woodrow Wilson, Abraham Lincoln, Barack Obama*

- ❖ **Common characteristic:** *Men who made significant changes to the United States of America*
- ❖ **Unique characteristic:** *First President under current Constitution, elected unanimously*
- ❖ **Definition:** *George Washington was the first President under the current Constitution and is the only President elected unanimously.*

Example E

- ❖ **Term:** *Kitchenmaid (from* The Nightingale*)*
- ❖ **Groups:** *Daughters, girls, workers,*
- ❖ **Choose a group:** *workers*
- ❖ **Other members of the group:** *The fisherman, the cavalier, the handmaids, cooks*
- ❖ **Common characteristic:** *Employed by the emperor for the purpose of serving him while earning a living*
- ❖ **Unique characteristic:** *Knew location of the bird; willing to show to the emperor*
- ❖ **Definition:** *The Kitchenmaid was a worker who knew the location of the bird and was willing to show it to the Emperor.*

Assessment
Confirm that students have:

- ✓ Completed one definition for each key term
- ✓ Moved any new information that fits the A or N column to their ANI chart

Tip:

Pay particular attention to the final Definition step:
Do their definitions make sense?

SAMPLE STUDENT WORKSHEET

Essay Five Invention
DEFINITION I

1. Identify a term from your issue.

_____

2. List three or four groups this term belongs to.

_____

3. Select a group from the list above which will be helpful for you as you define the term.

_____

4. List other members (three or four) of the group you selected.

_____
_____
_____
_____

5. Identify a common characteristic of all members of this group (What quality do all the members share?).

_____
_____
_____

6. What characteristic makes the term *different from these other group members?*

_____

7. Write your definition. Include the term, its group, and its difference. In other words, state that the term is a member of its group and how it is different from all the other members.

> ### EXAMPLES
>
> **Term:** blue whale
> **Group:** mammal
> **Difference:** largest known to have existed
> **Definition:** The blue whale is the largest mammal known to exist.
>
> **Term:** Mr. Tumnus
> **Group:** faun
> **Difference:** invited Lucy to tea
> **Definition:** Mr. Tumnus is a faun who invited Lucy to tea

Your Definition:
_____
_____
_____

Review your I column, and move any appropriate items to the A or N columns.

Essay Five Arrangement
DIVISION

Tools for the Teacher

Essay Five Arrangement Worksheets (page 53 in the Student Workbook)
Samples from this lesson guide for class discussion

Definitions

- **Division**
  A statement of the agreement and disagreement between the two sides of an argument or debate; it include a *common opinion, Thesis, and Counter-Thesis*

- **Distribution**
  The portion of the Division that includes the Thesis, Enumeration, and Exposition

- **Counter-thesis**
  The statement of the position in direct opposition to the Thesis

Background for the Teacher

- **Idea:** Division clarifies the agreement and disagreement in the argument.

- The Division is added to the Persuasive Essay Introduction. It defines the actual difference of opinion and minimizes the possibility that the two sides will argue about something on which they don't disagree. It also enables the audience to see where the two sides differ.

  Note: The Persuasive Essay Template changes in this lesson because a "Distribution" has been added to it, and the Thesis, Enumeration, and Exposition are placed in the Distribution.

Your Students Will Learn How to:

- ✓ State the Thesis and Counter-Thesis
- ✓ List common opinions of the opposing positions
- ✓ Choose one point of common agreement
- ✓ Add this Division information to the Arrangement Worksheet and Template

Steps to Teach This Lesson

☐ **Begin by raising to your students' awareness the need to clarify what the argument is actually about.** Your students have likely had an argument only to discover that they were actually talking about slightly different things or even that they didn't disagree after all. This happens a lot on the playground and in politics. Discuss this.

A Division statement begins to solve this problem.

☐ **Present several examples of generating a Division.** We have included several examples for you below, and it is also helpful to practice using issues from your students' work.

Each time you generate an example of Division, complete these steps:

- ❖ **Thesis:** Edmund should not follow the White Witch.

- ❖ **Counter-Thesis:** Edmund should follow the White Witch.

- ❖ **Common terms:** Edmund, follow, White Witch

- ❖ **Common opinion:**

    - ○ *Is there anything on which both sides agree?*
      Edmund had to make a decision, he could not stay where he was because he would freeze, he was lost, he was being offered something by the Queen of Narnia, he was away from everyone he knew, he needed help, he did follow the White Witch

    - ○ *Is there anything that both sides of the argument want?*
      To have Edmund make a decision

- **Choose one point of common agreement:** Edmund could not stay where he was.

- **Some people believe . . . (Thesis):** Edmund should not have followed the White Witch.

- **Conversely, other believe that . . . (Counter-Thesis):** Edmund should have followed the White Witch

Repeat this with several more examples.

Allow time for discussion and clarification. Students might pick a point of agreement that seems very general at first, and that is fine as long as it is a point of agreement. Trust that clarifying the actual distinction between two sides of an argument will take time as they grow in understanding and judgment.

☐ Once they understand the idea of finding and forming a Division, **show them its place in the Persuasive Essay Template**.

Template sample

I. Introduction
    A. Exordium
    B. Division

        1. Agreement: Edmund could not stay where he was
        2. Disagreement
            a) Some say he should follow
            b) Some say he should not follow
    C. Distribution
        1. Thesis: Edmund should not have followed the White Witch
        2. Enumeration: Three reasons
        3. Exposition
            a) Ignored a warning
            b) Overlooked the evil
            c) Acted in secret

☐ Ask the students to **compare the Divisions they completed**. Have them describe the steps taken, to explain the purpose of the Division, and state where the Division goes in the essay.

☐ **Assign** *Essay Five Arrangement: Division* Worksheet (page 53 in the Student Workbook) for their own essay. Then they will complete the Essay Five Worksheet (page 55) and Essay Five Arrangement Template page 58).

Examples

Example A
from "The Gift of the Magi"

- ❖ **Thesis:** Della should cut her hair.

- ❖ **Counter-Thesis:** Della should not cut her hair.

- ❖ **Common terms:** Hair, Della, Cut

- ❖ **Common opinion:**

    - ○ *Is there anything on which both sides agree?*
      No one would want to buy short hair because it is of no value to the buyer, Della's hair is a valuable commodity, she could certainly make money by selling her hair, she has very little money but wants to buy a good Christmas gift for her husband, her hair is unusually long and beautiful

- ○ *Is there anything that both sides of the argument want?*
  Both sides want to be able to give a gift to a love one at Christmas

- ❖ **Choose one point of common agreement:** Della wanted to earn money for a gift.

- ❖ **Some people believe . . . (Thesis):** Della should have cut her hair.

- ❖ **Conversely, others believe that . . . (Counter-Thesis):** Della should not have cut her hair

- ❖ **Template sample:**

    I. Introduction
       A. Exordium
       B. Division
           1. Agreement: earn money to give a gift
           2. Disagreement
               a. Some say she not have cut her hair
               b. Some say she should have cut her hair
       C. Distribution
           1. Thesis: Della should have cut her hair

  2. Enumeration: Three reasons
  3. Exposition
    a. Sacrifice
    b. Love
    c. Christmas

Example C
from The Odyssey

- **Thesis:** Odysseus should have killed the suitors.

- **Counter-Thesis:** Odysseus should not have killed the suitors

- **Common terms:** Odysseus, killed, suitor

- **Common opinion:**

    - *Is there anything on which both sides agree?*
      The suitors were breaking the tradition of Ancient Greek hospitality, Odysseus home and family had been taken advantage of

- *Is there anything that both sides of the argument want?*
  Justice, care of Odysseus' family

- **Choose one point of common agreement:** Odysseus needed to stop the suitors.

- **Some people believe . . . (Thesis):** Odysseus should have killed the suitors.

- **Conversely, others believe that . . . (Counter-Thesis):** Odysseus should not have killed the suitors.

- **Template sample:**

 I. Introduction
  A. Exordium
  B. Division
    1. Agreement: Needed to stop suitors
    2. Disagreement
      a) Should kill suitors

     b) Should not kill suitors
 C. Distribution
   1. Thesis: Odysseus should have killed the suitors
   2. Enumeration: Three reasons
   3. Exposition
     a) Odysseus' home
     b) Suitors' abuse
     c) Suitors' corruption

Assessment
Confirm that students have:

- ✓ Completed the Division Worksheet for their current essay

- ✓ Completed the Essay Five Arrangement Worksheet

- ✓ Transcribed the Arrangement Five Template for their current essay

SAMPLE STUDENT WORKSHEET

Essay Five Arrangement
DIVISION

Write your Thesis.
_____

Write your Counter-Thesis.
_____

Common Opinions

Regarding your issue, *it is commonly agreed that . . .*
_____
_____
_____
_____
_____
_____
_____

Is there anything that both sides want, fear, or believe?
_____
_____

Agreement

On what do both sides agree?

_____
_____
_____
_____
_____

Choose one point of agreement.

_____
_____
_____

Disagreement

Some people believe (Thesis):

_____
_____

Conversely, some other people believe (Counter-Thesis):

_____
_____

Essay Five Arrangement Template
BASIC PERSUASIVE ESSAY

Transcribe your outline onto a separate page, using the template provided below. Do not use complete sentences.

Replace lines that have an asterisk with *your* information from the Arrangement Worksheet on the previous pages.

I. Introduction
    A. Exordium*
    B. Division
        1. Agreement*
        2. Disagreement
            a. Thesis*
            b. Counter-Thesis*
    C. Distribution
        1. Thesis*
        2. Enumeration*
        3. Exposition
            a. Proof I*
            b. Proof II*
            c. Proof III*

II. Proof
    A. Proof I*
        1. Sub-Proof 1*
        2. Sub-Proof 2*
        3. Sub-Proof 3*
    B. Proof II*
        1. Sub-Proof 1*
        2. Sub-Proof 2*
        3. Sub-Proof 3*
    C. Proof III*
        1. Sub-Proof 1*
        2. Sub-Proof 2*
        3. Sub-Proof 3*

III. Conclusion
    A. Thesis*
    B. Summary of Proof
        3. Proof I*
        4. Proof II*
        5. Proof III*
    C. Amplification
        6. To whom it matters*
        7. Why it matters to that person or group*

Essay Five Elocution
ANTITHESIS

Tools for the Teacher
Essay Five Elocution Worksheet (page 59 in the Student Workbook)
Samples from this lesson guide for class discussion

Definitions

- ❖ **Antithesis:** Antithesis is a scheme in which strongly contrasting (or opposite) ideas are expressed in parallel form.

Background for the Teacher

- ❖ **Idea:** Antithesis juxtaposes two contrasting ideas in parallel form.

In Essay Two, your students learned how to write using parallel structure; for this lesson, they will learn a specific type of parallelism called antithesis.

Your students may find that the Comparison charts developed during Invention provide possible starting points to generate antithetical phrases. Adverbs are generally easy to find opposites for, as well.

We provide several examples for you to use. Noting additional examples of Antithesis in books, speeches, poetry, etc. will help cement this idea firmly in your students' minds.

Remember, antithesis can be expressed many different ways, sometimes parts of speech made exactly parallel, sometimes with a looser structure. Your students will become better at identifying and generating antithesis through experience and exposure, so keep it simple with this lesson.

Your Students Will Learn to:

✓ Define and Identify Antithesis
✓ Generate Antithesis
✓ Add Antithesis to their Persuasive Essay

Steps to Teach This Lesson

☐ **Begin** this lesson by writing words on the board such as, "sweet," "dark," "smooth," "loud," and have students give you words that mean the opposite. If you want, you could write some longer ideas such as, "joyous victory," "muffled whisper", or "rocky road", and have them list ideas that juxtapose these longer thoughts, such as, "bitter defeat," "raucous noise," or "grassy meadow."

☐ **Introduce** them to common sayings or proverbs that include antithesis. See if they can fill in the second half of these phrases:

- *To err is human....(to forgive, divine)*
- *Give me liberty....(or give me death)*

☐ **Present** an example of a sentence using Antithesis and the same without. What are the differences? What previously learned scheme is used in the first example below?

Example:

We must learn to live together as brothers or perish together as fools.
Vs.
We should really learn to live together, within our community, treating each other like brothers and sisters, because if we don't we are really acting foolish, and the end result would be that we would all perish.

☐ **Ask** them to describe antithesis. They should recognize that it is a pair of phrases or clauses written in parallel contrasting form.

☐ Next, **show** them how to create antithetical statements of their own. Their *Comparison: Differences* worksheets provide opposite ideas that they can practice with. It is often relatively easy to find opposites for adverbs and prepositions, as well.

Find a phrase or clause in your writing for which you can create a contrasting phrase or clause.

- *Edmund considered the Turkish Delight*
- *Peter was a responsible leader*
- *Edmund was cold, hungry and afraid*

Generate a contrasting phrase, or clause.

- *While the Witch plotted against Aslan*
- *But Edmund was an impudent loner*
- *While the White Witch was warm, able to make food, and very powerful*

Make the second idea parallel to the first and rewrite your sentence using these two contrasting ideas in parallel form.

- *Edmund considered Turkish Delight while the Witch plotted against Aslan.*
- *Peter was a responsible leader but Edmund was an impudent loner.*
- *Edmund was cold hungry and afraid while the White Witch was warm, able to make food, and very powerful.*

After writing several sentences with antithesis, ask students to **compare** the process they took each time.

- What steps did you take to create antithesis?
- How did you start?
- What are some contrasting words you used?
- How did you come up with a contrasting phrase or clause?
- What structure did you use to write your antithesis?

☐ **Assign** Essay Five Elocution Worksheet: Antithesis (page 59 in the Student Workbook). Students will also add an example of antithesis to their essay this week.

Examples

❖ From Jim McCay, Sportscaster:

  "The thrill of victory, the agony of defeat."

❖ From Martin Luther King Junior's speech in St. Louis, 1964:

"We must learn to live together as brothers or perish together as fools."

- From Shakespeare's *The Tragedy of Julius Caesar*:

    "Not that I loved Caesar less, but that I loved Rome more."

- From Charles Dickens' *A Tale of Two Cities*:

    "It was the best of times, it was the worst of times, it was the age of wisdom, it was the age of foolishness, it was the epoch of belief, it was the epoch of incredulity, it was the season of Light, it was the season of Darkness, it was the spring of hope, it was the winter of despair, we had everything before us, we had nothing before us, we were all going direct to Heaven, we were all going direct the other way."

- From Abraham Lincoln's "The Gettysburg Address", 1863:

    "The world will little note, nor long remember what we say here, but it can never forget what they did here."

- From Geoffrey Chaucer's *The Wife of Bath's Prologue*:

    *"Mercury stands for wisdom, thrift and science,
    Venus for revel, squandering, and defiance."*

Assessment
Confirm that students have:

- ✓ Completed *Essay Five Elocution: Antithesis* Worksheet
- ✓ Added Antithesis to their current essay
- ✓ Written Essay Five, following the Essay Five checklist

SAMPLE STUDENT WORKSHEET

Essay Five Elocution
ANTITHESIS

Definition

Antithesis is a scheme in which strongly contrasting (or opposite) ideas are expressed in parallel form.

Examples

From Neil Armstrong's Moon Landing Speech

"That's one **small step for man**; one **giant leap for mankind.**"

From Alexander Pope's *An Essay on Criticism*

"To err is human; to forgive divine."

From Martin Luther King, Jr.'s *I Have a Dream* Speech

"I have a dream that my four little children will one day live in a nation where they will not be judged **by the color of their skin** but **by the content of their character.** I have a *dream* today!"

From Charles Dicken's *A Tale of Two Cities*

"It was the **best** of times, it was the **worst** of times, it was the age of **wisdom**, it was the age of **foolishness**, it was the epoch of ***belief***, it was the epoch of ***incredulity***, it was the season of **Light**, it was the season of **Darkness**, it was ***the spring of hope***, it was ***the winter of despair***, we had **everything** before us, we had **nothing** before us, we were all going direct to ***Heaven***, we were all going direct ***the other way***."

Steps to Creating Antithesis

1. Find an idea in your writing for which you can create a contrasting phrase or clause. *Edmund should not follow the White Witch.*
2. Generate a contrasting phrase or clause. *He should follow Lucy.*
3. Make the second idea parallel to the first and rewrite your sentence using these two contrasting ideas in parallel form. *Edmund should not follow the White Witch. However, he should follow Lucy.*

Student Examples

Edmund was a confused, lost boy, while the White Witch was a conniving, plotting ruler.

Edmund hoped for power, but settled for promises.

Though Odysseus accomplished his own homecoming, his crew lost their lives.

He lived in weakness but died in strength.

The sacrifice of the few provides for the prosperity of many.

The tragedy of the many reveals the greed of a few.

Practice

Write a sentence using antithesis about someone you respect, such as a family member or a friend.

Find an idea to emphasize.

_____

Generate contrasting ideas (words or phrases).

_____

Select a contrasting idea that emphasizes your original idea.

_____

Make the second idea parallel to the first, and rewrite your sentence using these two contrasting ideas in parallel form.

_____

Next, write a sentence using antithesis about something you can see outside.

Find an idea to emphasize.

_____

Generate contrasting ideas (words or phrases).

_____

Select a contrasting idea that emphasizes your original idea.

_____

Make the second idea parallel to the first, and rewrite your sentence using these two contrasting ideas in parallel form.

_____

Write a sentence using antithesis about a character in a favorite book.

Find an idea to emphasize.
_____

Generate contrasting ideas (words or phrases).
_____

Select a contrasting idea that emphasizes your original idea.
_____

Make the second idea parallel to the first and rewrite your sentence using these two contrasting ideas in parallel form.
_____
_____

Now add your own examples of antithesis to Essay Five.

ESSAY SIX

Essay Six Invention
CIRCUMSTANCE

Tools for the Teacher

Essay Five Invention Worksheet (page 65 in the Student Workbook)
Samples from this lesson guide for class discussion

Definitions

- ❖ **Circumstance:** One of the Five Common Topics, Circumstance describes the actions and events that occur at the same time as, but in different locations from, the situation in which the issue arises.

- ❖ **Situation:** The setting, actors, and dilemma in which the Issue arises. The situation is developed much further in the lessons on Narratio and Relation.

Background for the Teacher

- ❖ **Idea:** The Topic of Circumstance is used to generate information about actions and events that occur at the same time as, but in different places from, the situation in which the issue must be decided.

- ❖ Circumstance helps your students gather information about the context in which the Issue must be decided, both in place and time.

- ❖ Circumstance seeks out what is happening in these locations at the same time as the situation, but you should not be too precise about the time parameter. Let students use and develop their common sense. Focus on the places surrounding the Issue and what is happening there at about the same time. In short, the Topic of Circumstance is concerned primarily with place, while The Topic of Relation discovers events in time.

❖ As with all Topics of Invention, information generated through the Topic of Circumstance is considered part of the I column. Your students will move any fitting information to the Affirmative and Negative columns.

Remember that the Invention lessons always start a new essay, and the skills learned in previous lesson are practiced again for each new essay. Students begin a new essay by forming a new Issue and starting a new ANI.

Your Students Will Learn How to:

✓ Discover the Circumstances surrounding the situation in which the Issue must be decided.

- *What was happening in the same place?*
- *What was happening in the surrounding locations?*
- *What was happening anywhere else students choose to explore?*

Steps to Teach This Lesson

☐ **Discuss** how often what is going on at the time of any decision influences that decision. Start with examples from the students' lives.

- *When they are faced with the decision to get out of bed in the morning, what else is going on?*

- *When they must decide whether to get up from the couch and load the dishwasher, what is the situation?*

- *What else is going on at that time?*

☐ **Model and practice** several examples of Circumstance with your students. Several examples are included in this lesson and use other past issues or new issues from your literature/history studies.

> **Teaching Tip**
>
> For this Essay, your students will also complete Definition and Comparison worksheets to gather information for the issue generated in this lesson. They are collecting new tools for their Tool Boxes and continuing to practice each of them.

- *Write your Issue*

- Describe the situation (the time and location in which an issue needs to be decided).

- Use the chart in the Student Workbook (we have listed several examples below) to list actions and events that occur at the same time but in different locations surrounding your issue.

- Move information from the Circumstance worksheet to the A and N columns as appropriate.

❖ **Issue:** *Whether Edmund should have followed the White Witch*

❖ **Situation***: Winter in Narnia, Edmund is cold*

❖ **List actions and events that occur at the same time but in different locations surrounding your issue:**

- *1st place*: Lucy is with the beavers who are telling her about Aslan, the Narnians are suffering, Edmund is lost and cold

- *2nd place:* Peter and Susan are back in the professor's house, professor is working

- *3rd place*: Europe: WWII, Their mother is in London, and their father is off to war

There are no set "locations" for each circle on the Circumstance chart. Start by thinking about the place the actor is in when making this decision and move out from there. This is Invention, so don't feel bound to circumstances that are obviously affecting this Issue. Invention is for discovery, so encourage your students to send their minds exploring.

☐ **Review** the steps and questions used in Circumstance.
What is the situation of the issue? What did you list in the first circle each time? What did you list in the next circle? What did you list in the last circle? In each example, what did you do with this new information?

☐ **Assign** the Essay Six Invention Worksheet (page 65 in the Student Workbook) for the new essay.

Examples

Example A
from "The Gift of the Magi"

- ❖ **Issue:** Whether Della should cut her hair

- ❖ **Situation:** early 1900's, Christmas season, most likely New York City, her apartment

- ❖ **List actions and events that occur at the same time but in different locations surrounding your Issue:**
    - *1st place:* Neighbors across the way might be hanging laundry and looking out their window, Della is thinking about Christmas, Della fixing her long hair, Della is reminded of how simple the apartment is

    - *2nd place: (around the town)* City shopkeepers putting Christmas decorations in windows, Mme. Sofronie's works at her shop "Hair Goods, Bought and Sold", Mme. Sofronie examines hair, Jim is considering buying combs for Della, Jim at work

    - *3rd place:* Americans working and keeping up their own homes, Many people are likely preparing for Christmas, some Americans have great wealth, many have great poverty

---

Example B
from The Odyssey

- ❖ **Issue:** Whether Odysseus should listen to the sirens

- ❖ **Situation:** When they pass the sirens

- ❖ **List actions and events that occur at the same time but in different locations surrounding your Issue:**

- *1st place:* Odysseus and crewmen passing by, deciding about listening, remembering warnings
- *2nd place:* Penelope and Telemachos worrying about her husband (his father), hoping he's home soon, dealing with the suitors every day

- *3rd place:* Mount Olympus and the gods, seeing what Odysseus will do, engaged in their own petty arguments

---

Assessment
Confirm that students:

- ✓ Have completed the Essay Six Invention: Circumstance Worksheet for the current essay

- ✓ Have moved any relevant points from the Circumstance Worksheet to their ANI charts

SAMPLE STUDENT WORKSHEET

Essay Six Invention
CIRCUMSTANCE

Write your Issue.

_____

Describe the situation (the time and location in which your Issue needs to be decided).

_____

Use the chart below to list actions and events that occur at the same time as, in different locations from, your Issue.

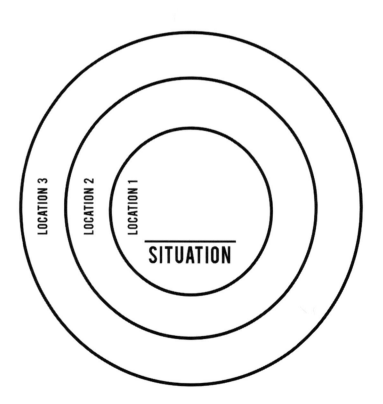

Essay Six Arrangement
REFUTATION

Tools for the Teacher

Essay Six Arrangement Worksheets (page 66 in the Student Workbook)
Samples from this lesson guide for class discussion

Definitions

- **Refutation:** The response to an opposing argument. For the persuasive essay, you anticipate two arguments that your opponent will have against your Thesis. A Refutation states those two Counter-Proofs and why they are inadequate.

- **Counter-Thesis:** The proposition that states the opposite of the Thesis

- **Counter-Proofs:** The Proofs that support the Counter-Thesis

Background for the Teacher

- **Idea:** Refutation presents the opposing side's Counter-Thesis and two strong Counter-Proofs, states what is wrong with each, and concludes by stating that the Counter-Thesis is not persuasive.

- It is a moral imperative that students learn to respect both the act of argumentation/decision-making and the position of those with whom they argue. Refutation is a means to cultivate that respect.

- Having said that, this is the students' first formal introduction to a Refutation, so they should not be expected to exercise profound judgment. The goal in this lesson is simply to introduce the concept.

Your Students Will Learn to:

- ✓ Select two strong proofs for the opposing argument
- ✓ Determine why the Counter-Proofs are insufficient
- ✓ Express that those Counter-Proofs are insufficient to overcome the Thesis

Steps to Teach This Lesson

☐ **Ask your students** if they felt their opponent understood their position in a recent argument about whether to do something. Then ask if they try as hard to understand the opposing argument as they do to express their own ideas. Ask, "Does that work well?"

Ask whether we make our own case better when we know why others oppose our idea, or when we don't know their reasons.

☐ **Model and present several clear examples** of forming a Refutation. We have several examples below, and you should take examples from class ANIs and past persuasive essay work.

The Refutation expands the ideas begun with the Division. There, students learned to acknowledge the opposing side and specify the point of disagreement between the Thesis and Counter-Thesis. By adding a Refutation, students directly address two Counter-Proofs that support the Counter-Thesis.

When your students developed and sorted their ANI charts, they already developed the Counter-Proofs. Encourage them to select two strong Counter-Proofs and then determine why they are inadequate to overcome the Thesis. You could ask them, "Why did you not choose that side when you decided on your thesis?"

Steps to creating a Refutation

- Write your Thesis statement.

- Write the Counter-Thesis.

- Choose one proof that supports the Counter-Thesis. This becomes the Counter-Proof.

- List three Sub-Proofs (members of that group).

- Explain why this Proof is not persuasive.

- Choose a second Proof for the Counter-Thesis and repeat the steps above.

Example

1. Write your Thesis statement: *Edmund should not follow the White Witch.*

2. Write your Counter-Thesis: *Edmund should follow the White Witch.*

3. Choose one strong Proof (from your sorted groups) that supports the Counter-Thesis: *White Witch cared about Edmund*

4. List three Sub-Proofs (members of that group):
   - *Took care of him*
   - *Spoke kindly to him*
   - *Fed him*

5. Explain why this Proof is not persuasive: *All of these actions were simply means to trick and tempt Edmund.*

6. Choose a second strong Proof for the counter-thesis and repeat the steps above. *Edmund was distressed and distracted*

7. List three Sub-Proofs (members of that group):
   - *Alone*
   - *Scared*
   - *Too cold to think*

8. Explain why this Proof is not persuasive: *He wasn't really alone, Lucy and other allies were with him in Narnia*

To prevent the Refutation from growing out of proportion to the rest of the essay, be sure to limit it to the two Counter-Proofs and Sub-Counter-Proofs described on the outline.

☐ Ask your students to **compare the steps** you took each time you created a Refutation.

- *What was your starting point? (my own Thesis)*
- *How did you form the Counter-Thesis each time? (negated my Thesis)*
- *Where did you find the Counter-Proofs?*

- *How did you finish each Refutation?*

☐ **Assign** Essay Six Arrangement Worsheet: Refutation (page 66 in the Student Workbook) for their essay. Then they will complete the Essay Six Worksheet (page 68) and Essay Six Arrangement Template (page 72).

Examples

Example A
from "Gift of the Magi"

- ❖ **Thesis:** Della should cut her hair

- ❖ **Counter Thesis:** Della should not cut her hair

- ❖ **Choose one Proof that supports the Counter-Thesis:** Jim's probable reaction

- ❖ *List three sub-proofs (members of that group):*
    - Might not like her with short hair
    - Might feel bad about receiving a gift that cost her her hair
    - Short-haired wife might hurt his career

- ❖ **Explain why this Proof is not persuasive:** Jim's willingness to sacrifice his own most valuable possession shows us that he loves his wife very much. There's no evidence to convince us he would suddenly turn against Della.

- ❖ **List a Proof for the Counter-Thesis:** Couple's budget

- ❖ *List three Sub-Proofs (members of that group):*
    - Jim wears a shabby coat
    - Salary reduction
    - Barely enough money to buy food

- ❖ **Explain why this Proof is not persuasive:** Although they are currently in need of extra money, they have been able to support themselves adequately. Della manages to serve chops for Christmas dinner. A special occasion calls for a special gift.

Example B
from Anne of Green Gables

- ❖ **Thesis:** Anne should go away to college

- ❖ **Counter-Thesis:** Anne should not go away to college

- ❖ **Choose one Proof that supports the Counter-Thesis:** Marilla needs her at home

- ❖ *List three Sub-Proofs (members of that group):*
    - o Anne helps with farm work
    - o Helps with kitchen work
    - o Provides company

- ❖ **Explain why this Proof is not persuasive:** Marilla herself thinks college is what Anne needs

- ❖ **List another Proof for the Counter-Thesis:** Gilbert wants Anne to stay where he is

- ❖ *List three Sub-Proofs (members of that group):*
    - o They've known each other a long time
    - o He likes her
    - o He may propose if she's there

- ❖ **Explain why this Proof is not persuasive:** Anne has no reason to commit to Gilbert at this point

---

Example C
from The Hobbit

- ❖ **Thesis:** Bilbo should give the ring to Frodo

- ❖ **Counter-Thesis:** Bilbo should not give the ring to Frodo

- ❖ **Choose one Proof that supports the Counter-Thesis:** Bilbo really wants to keep the ring

- ❖ *List three Sub-Proofs (members of that group):*
    - o *it gives comfort to him*
    - o *he's used to wearing it*

- *would miss it*

- ❖ **Explain why this Proof is not persuasive:** What we want may not be what's best for us

- ❖ **List another Proof for the Counter-Thesis:** Bilbo has suffered no harm from owning the ring so far

- ❖ *List three Sub-Proofs (members of that group):*
  - he's happy with the ring
  - it belongs to him
  - he's healthy

- ❖ **Explain why this Proof is not persuasive:** There is evidence that Bilbo is beginning to feel the effects of the Ring's dark power

---

Example D
from The Iliad

- ❖ **Thesis:** Agamemnon should not take Briseis from Achilles

- ❖ **Counter-Thesis:** Agamemnon should take Briseis from Achilles

- ❖ **Choose one Proof that supports the Counter-Thesis:** Agamemnon is leader of the armies and therefore has the power, privilege, and responsibility

- ❖ *List three Sub-Proofs (members of that group):*
  - he has power
  - privileges
  - responsibilities

- ❖ **Explain why this Proof is not persuasive:** His position as a leader doesn't justify taking what he wants from others.

- ❖ **List another Proof for the Counter-Thesis:** Achilles defied Agamemnon.

- ❖ *List three sub-proofs (members of that group):*
  - Achilles was enraged
  - embarrassed the king
  - angered the king

❖ **Explain why this Proof is not persuasive:** One can't take what's not one's own just because someone made you angry

---

Assessment
Confirm that students have:

- ✓ Completed the Refutation Worksheet
- ✓ Completed the Essay Six Arrangement Worksheet
- ✓ Transcribed the Arrangement Six Template

SAMPLE STUDENT WORKSHEET

Essay Six Arrangement A
GUIDE TO REFUTATION

Write your Thesis statement.
_____

Write your Counter-Thesis.
_____

Choose one Proof that supports the Counter-Thesis.
_____

List three Sub-Proofs.
_____
_____
_____

Explain why this Proof is not persuasive.
_____
_____
_____

Choose a second Proof for the Counter-Thesis.
_____

Choose three Sub-Proofs.
_____
_____
_____

Explain why this Proof is not persuasive.
___
___
___

Essay Six Arrangement Template
BASIC PERSUASIVE ESSAY

Transcribe your outline onto a separate page, imitating the template provided below. Do not use complete sentences. Replace lines that have an asterisk with your information from the Arrangement Worksheet on the previous pages.

I. Introduction
    A. Exordium*
    B. Division
        1. Agreement*
        2. Disagreement
            a. Thesis*
            b. Counter-Thesis*
    C. Distribution
        1. Thesis*
        2. Enumeration*
        3. Exposition
            a. Proof I*
            b. Proof II*
            c. Proof III*

II. Proof
    A. Proof I*
        1. Sub-Proof 1*
        2. Sub-Proof 2*
        3. Sub-Proof 3*
    B. Proof II*
        1. Sub-Proof 1*
        2. Sub-Proof 2*
        3. Sub-Proof 3*
    C. Proof III*
        1. Sub-Proof 1*
        2. Sub-Proof 2*
        3. Sub-Proof 3*

III. Refutation
    A. Counter-Thesis*
    B. Counter-Proof 1*
        1. Summary of support for reason 1*
        2. Inadequacy of reason 1*
    C. Counter-Proof 2*
        1. Summary of support for reason 2 *
        2. Inadequacy of reason 2*
    D. Summary of Refutation*

IV. Conclusion
    A. Thesis*
    B. Summary of Proof
        1. Proof I*
        2. Proof II*
        3. Proof III*
    C. Amplification
        1. To whom it matters*
        2. Why it matters*

Essay Six Elocution

SIMILE

Tools for the Teacher

Essay Six Elocution Worksheet (page 73 in the Student Workbook)
Samples from this lesson guide for class discussion

Definitions

- **Simile:** Simile is a trope that makes an explicit comparison of two things different in kind but sharing a common characteristic. It uses words as "like" or "as" to make the comparison.

- **Trope:** A figure of speech that appeals to the mind or imagination

---

Background for the Teacher

- **Idea:** A simile is an explicit comparison of two things that are of a different kind but share a quality.

Your Students Will Learn to:

✓ Define a simile
✓ Identify similes
✓ Generate similes and add them to their essays

Steps to Teach This Lesson

☐ **Review** the topic of Comparison: Similarities.

Here are some sample questions to get you started.

- o *How can we compare things?*
- o *What do you look for when you compare things?*

☐ **Present** several examples of similes. We have provided several in the section below. You can find many more in books, article, on-line or even in common speech. Clichés are often similes that work like a charm, so they become overused and lose their impact.

Ask the students to compare the examples to each other. Add some simple comparisons as well, so they see that not every comparison is a simile. "Tom is like Larry" is not a simile.

> ### Teaching Tip
> Remember that if you compare the same kinds of things !e.g. two animals, such as a cat and a dog" you create a simple comparison, not a simile. A simile MUST be a comparison between different kinds of things.

☐ Next **teach** your students how to generate their own similes.

Here's how:

- *Write the term.*

- *Select a characteristic or quality of this term.*

- *Choose a different kind of thing that shares this characteristic and join it to your first term with a comparative word such as "like" or "as". In addition, the verbs "is" "has" and "does" can help generate similes just as they helped generate comparisons earlier.*

Similes come in two common forms:

- X is as Adjective as Y
- X is like Y

Experiment with these forms, using the verbs "have" and "do" as well.

Example 1

Write the term to describe with a simile:
Bird

List 4-5 characteristics or qualities of this term:
loud, beautiful, feathered, singer, loud-squawker

Choose a different kind of thing that shares one of these **characteristics and** join it to your first term with a comparative word such as "like" or "as":
The bird is like a train ("is")
The bird is as loud as a train ("is as adjective as...")
Like a train rumbling down the tracks, the bird's squawking goes on and on (does)

<u>Not a simile: The Mockingbird chanted like a Nightingale</u>

Example 2

Write the term that you'd like to describe with a simile:
my cat

List 4-5 characteristics or qualities of this term:
aggressive, psychotic, independent, fast

Choose a different kind of thing that shares one of these **characteristics and** join it to your first term with a comparative word such as "like" or "as":
My cat is like a heat-seeking missile .
My cat is as fast as a bullet.

<u>Not a simile: My cat is as fast as a cheetah.</u>

☐ Ask the students to explain in their own words the steps you took to create similes, comparing how you did it each time.

☐ Assign *Elocution Six Worksheet: Simile* (page 73 in the Student Workbook).

☐ Ask the students to add one or more similes to their essays following the pattern you taught in class.

Examples

- ❖ From Proverbs 11:22:

    "***As a jewel of gold*** *in a swine's snout, so is* ***a fair woman*** *which is without discretion.*"

- ❖ From John Steinbeck's *Of Mice and Men*:

    "*Curley was* ***flopping like a fish*** *on a line.*"

- ❖ From Shakespeare's *Sonnet CXLVII*:

    "***My love is as a fever****, longing still*
    For that which longer nurseth the disease."

- ❖ From Psalm 42:1:

    "***As the hart panteth*** *after the water brooks,*
    so panteth my soul *after thee, O God.*"

Assessment
Confirm that students have:

- ✓ Completed Essay Six Elocution: Simile Worksheet
- ✓ Added simile to their current essay
- ✓ Written Essay Six, referring to the Essay Six checklist for self-editing

SAMPLE STUDENT WORKSHEET

Essay Six Elocution
SIMILE

Definition

Simile is a trope that makes an explicit comparison of two things different in kind but sharing a common characteristic. Similes use "like," "as," or "seems" to make a comparison explicit.

Examples

From Psalm 42:1

"As the hart panteth after the water brooks, so panteth my soul after thee, O God."

From Proverbs 11:22

"As a jewel of gold in a swine's snout, so is a fair woman which is without discretion."

From C.S. Lewis's *The Lion, the Witch, and the Wardrobe*

"Edmund saw the drop for a second in midair, shining like a diamond."

From Homer's *The Iliad*

"Like a man in his helplessness who, crossing a great plain, stands at the edge of a fast-running river that dashes seaward, and watches it thundering into white water, and leaps a pace backward, so now Tydeus' son gave back."

From Homer's *The Iliad*

"Like some ox of the herd pre-eminent among the others, a bull, who stands conspicuous in the huddling cattle; such was the son of Atreus as Zeus made him that day."

Steps to Creating Similes

1. Write the term that you'd like to describe with a simile. *Example: bird*

2. Select a characteristic or quality of this term.
   Examples: loud, beautiful, feathered, singer, loud-squawker

3. Choose a different kind of thing that shares this characteristic and join it to your first term with a comparative word such as "like" or "as".

   Examples: The bird is like a train / The bird is as loud as a train / Like a train rumbling down the tracks, the bird's squawking goes on and on.

Student Examples

The bird is like a train. OR The bird is as loud as a train.

My cat is like a pillow. OR My cat is as fluffy as a pillow.

> The mountains are like medicine for my soul.

> As the Emperor lay ill, Death sat as a heavy weight on his chest, tormenting him with mocking visions of the Emperor's wrongs in life and taking away his treasures: his sword, his banner, his crown, and now his life.

Practice

1. Choose something you can see and hold and describe it using simile.

    Term: _____

    Quality: _____

    Thing of a different kind that shares one quality:
    _____

    Simile:
    _____

2. Write a simile about a character in a book.

    Term: _____

    Quality: _____

    Thing of a different kind that shares one quality:
    _____

    Simile:
    _____

3. Practice writing several similes for terms from your essay.

   Term: _____

   Quality: _____

   Thing of a different kind that shares one quality:
   _____

   Simile:

   _____

   Now add your own examples of simile to Essay Six.

ESSAY SEVEN

Essay Seven Invention
RELATION

Tools for the Teacher

Essay Seven Invention Worksheet (page 79 in the Student Workbook)
Samples from this lesson guide for class discussion

Definitions

- ❖ **Relation:** One of the Five Common Topics, Relation lists events or actions that take place before and after the situation in which the issue arises and determines which are causes of the situation and which could be the effects of the actor's decisions (for or against).

Background for the Teacher

- ❖ **Idea:** Using the Common Topic of Relation, students generate information about the Issue by listing events and actions that precede and follow the situation. Some of the preceding events will be causes. Some of the following events will arise from the affirmative decision and some from the negative.

- ❖ Invention lessons always start a new essay and the skills from previous lessons are repeated for each new essay. Students will generate a new Issue and ANI.

- ❖ As with previous Invention Topics, all the information generated through the Topic of Relation should be considered part of the I column.

- ❖ After students generate information from the Topic of Relation they move any appropriate information to the Affirmative and Negative columns.

Your Students Will Learn to:

- ✓ Discover actions and events that preceded the situation, determine which are causes, and discover actions and events that follow either the Negative or Affirmative decision.

- ✓ To apply these questions to both the affirmative and then negative sides of their issue.

Steps to Teach This Lesson

☐ **Discuss** with your students how actions and events have causes and effects. Help them see that not everything that precedes an event causes it. Also, help them see that decisions bring about different effects.

First, ask students to identify an action or event they participated in or experienced (i.e. scoring a goal in a soccer game). Ask them what happened before the event. Make sure they list both causes and antecedents (things that just happened to precede the event). Then ask which items on the list contributed to the event as a cause and what simply happened beforehand but did not cause it (kicking a ball causes it to fly; the crowd buying hot dogs does not).

> ***Teaching Tip***
> You should also assign the students Definition, Comparison and Circumstance worksheets for their new issue.

Next, ask them to identify a recent decision they have made. Ask them what might have happened differently if they had made the opposite decision. Ask what happened because of the decision they made.

☐ **Model and present** several examples of Relation. We have included several examples below. Also discuss issues from literature and/or history sources.

- ✓ Write an issue.

- ✓ Describe the situation in which the actor finds himself.

- ✓ List several actions or events that preceded the situation.

- ✓ Select and circle several causes or probable causes of the situation.

- ✓ List several actions or events that followed or will likely follow the Affirmative decision.

- ✓ List several actions or events that followed or will likely follow the Negative decision.

- ✓ Select and circle several effects of probable effects of each decision.

☐ **Review** each of the steps.

- *What is the starting point for finding Relations? i.e. what do you need if you want to look for causes and effects? (a situation or Issue)*
- *How did you start each time? (identified the Issue)*
- *What did you describe next?*
- *What lists did you create each time?*
- *What did you go back and circle in each example?*
- *How will you use the Topic of Relation to generate information for your next essay?*

Each student should be able to articulate the process of generating information through the Topic of Relation.

☐ **Assign** the Essay Seven Invention Worksheet (page 79 of the Student Workbook).

Examples

Example A
from The Lion, the Witch, and the Wardrobe

- ❖ **Write your Issue** *Whether Edmund should have followed the White Witch*

- ❖ **Describe the situation in which the actor finds himself.** *Edmund is in Narnia, cold, hungry, alone, and lost.*

- ❖ **List several actions or events that preceded (or led up to) this situation.**
  - Edmund and his siblings had to move in with the professor.
  - The Nazis bombed London.
  - Edmund had a fight with his siblings.
  - The White Witch took over Narnia and made it perpetually winter.

- ❖ **Select and circle several causes or probable causes of the situation.**

- ❖ **List several actions or events that followed or will likely follow the Affirmative decision.**
  - Edmund was in danger.
  - The White Witch made him her minion.
  - Edmund gave up valuable information about Lucy's Narnian friends.
  - Edmund got more Turkish Delight.

- ❖ **List several actions or events that followed or will likely follow the Negative decision.**
  - Edmund would still have been very cold and hungry.
  - The witch wouldn't have been able to use Edmund.
  - The White Witch would have been very angry.
  - Edmund might have suffer terribly.

- ❖ **Select and circle several effects or probable effects of each decision.**

Example B
from "The Gift of the Magi"

- ❖ **Write your Issue** Whether Della should cut her hair

- ❖ **Describe the situation in which the actor finds himself.** She sees Madame Sofronie's shop that has a sign announcing the purchasing of hair.

- ❖ **List several actions or events that preceded this situation.**
  - Della wants to buy Jim a Christmas present.
  - Della does not have enough money to buy Jim a gift.
  - Della's hair is worth a lot of money.

- ❖ **Select and circle several causes or probable causes of the situation.**

- ❖ **List several actions or events that followed or will likely follow the Affirmative decision.**
  - Jim would not like it.
  - Della would be unhappy with her short hair.
  - Della would not have the option to sell her hair later when they need the money.

- Della would make enough money to buy Jim a nice gift.
- Jim would be happy because she gave him a gift.

❖ **List several actions or events that followed or will likely follow the Negative decision.**
- Della would not have a gift for Jim by Christmas.
- Della would keep her hair.
- Madame Sofronie would have to find a new seller.
- She would be able to use the combs that Jim will give her on Christmas.

❖ **Select and circle several effects or probable effects of each decision.**

Example C
from The Nightingale

❖ **Write your Issue:** Whether the Emperor should have received the artificial bird

❖ **Describe the situation in which the actor finds himself.** As the Emperor of China, he received an unexpected gift from the Emperor of Japan.

❖ **List several actions or events that preceded (or led up to) this situation.**

- All of the Emperor's subjects had already fallen in love with the song of the Nightingale.
  The kitchen-maid brought the Nightingale to the palace.
- The world acknowledged that the Nightingale was the best of all.
- The Nightingale sang gloriously for the Emperor, moving him to tears and touching his heart.
- The Nightingale relished the praise of the Emperor.
- The subjects of the land tried to sing just like the Nightingale but could not.

❖ **Select and circle several causes or probable causes of the situation.**

❖ **List several actions or events that followed or will likely follow the Affirmative decision**
- The Nightingale flew away out of the open window.

- The artificial bird sang its waltzes over and over again for the Emperor and his people.
- The two birds did not sing well together.
- The artificial bird had its place on a silken cushion by the Emperor's bed.
- The artificial bird received gold and precious stones, and a new title.
- All the people learned to sing the artificial bird's song by heart.
- The artificial bird's singing was more predictable than the Nightingale.

❖ **List several actions or events that followed or will likely follow the Negative decision**

- The Nightingale would have flown away.
- The Nightingale would not have been banished from the Kingdom.
- The Nightingale would have been around to continue singing for the Emperor and his people.
- The Emperor might not have gotten sick.
- The artificial bird would have been returned to the Emperor of Japan.

❖ **Select and circle several effects or probable effects of each decision**

Example D
from The Iliad

❖ **Write your Issue:** Whether Achilleus should have rejected Agamemnon's request to help the Greeks fight the Trojans.

❖ **Describe the situation in which the actor finds himself.**
Achilleus was robbed of Briseis and, therefore, of the honor and reward he feels was due him for his bravery and performance in battle

❖ **List several actions or events that preceded (or led up to) this situation.**
- Agamemnon took away Achilleus' honor.
- Agamemnon took Briseis (Achilleus' prize from a previous battle) away from Achilleus.
- Agamemnon severely insulted Achilleus.
- Achilleus' mother said he could sail back home.
- Fighting put Patroklos' life in danger.
- Agamemnon offered Achillieus gifts, including the return of Briseis to him.

- He respected the three warriors who came to persuade him to rejoin the battle.
- The Greeks were losing the battle and needed his help.
- Aias accused him of not caring about the fate of his fellow soldiers.
- Achilleus was a strong, fearless and formidable warrior.

❖ **Select and circle several causes or probable causes of the situation.**

❖ **List several actions or events that followed or will likely follow the Affirmative decision.**
- Agamemnon kept Briseis.
- The Trojans continued to win in battle.
- Most of the Greek leaders were wounded in battle.
- Conflict ensued among the gods.
- Patroklos died.

❖ **List several actions or events that followed or will likely follow the Negative decision.**
- The battle would have turned around in the Greeks' favor
- He might have prevented Patroklos' death
- He would have received the gifts offered to him
- He might have reconciled with Agamemnon
- He might have regained his sense of honor

❖ **Select and circle several effects or probable effects of each decision.**

Assessment
Confirm that students have:

- ✓ Completed the Essay 7 Invention: Relation Worksheet, pg.79
- ✓ Moved any relevant points from the Relation Worksheet to their ANI charts

SAMPLE STUDENT WORKSHEET

Essay Seven Invention
RELATION: CAUSE & EFFECT

Write your Issue.

_____

1. Describe the situation in which the actor finds himself.

_____

2. List several actions or events that preceded this situation.

_____
_____
_____
_____
_____
_____

3. Select and circle several causes or probable causes of the situation.

4. List several actions or events that followed or will likely follow the Affirmative decision.

_____
_____
_____
_____

5. List several actions or events that followed or will likely follow the Negative decision.

_____

_____

_____

_____

_____

6. Select and circle several effects or probable effects of each decision.

**Review your I column, and move
any appropriate items to the A or N.**

Essay Seven Arrangement
NARRATIO

Tools for the Teacher

Essay Seven Arrangement Worksheets (page 81 in Student Workbook)
Samples from this lesson guide for class discussion

Definitions

- **Setting:** When and where the story behind the Issue takes place

- **Actor:** The main characters involved

- **Action:** What the characters do

- **Cause:** The actions, events, etc. that brought about the situation

- **Effect:** The result of a decision, word, or deed

- **Situation:** The context in which the actor of your Issue must make (or has made) the decision. The situation includes the setting, the actors, any action or event taking place in the setting (i.e. a dance, game, battle, etc.), and the dilemma confronted by the main actor.

Background for the Teacher

- **Idea:** The Narratio is the "statement of facts" or the context which leads to the Issue in question.

- The outline of the Narratio will be added to the Introduction in the Persuasive Essay Template.

- Students will often wonder if the Narratio should be added to an existing paragraph or written as its own paragraph. There is no rule for this but propriety, so you should help your students determine what is appropriate based primarily on purpose, proportion, and integrity.

❖ **Why do we need the Narratio?**
Imagine trying to follow an argument about a certain issue without knowing who is involved, how the crisis arose, or even what possible decisions are open to the unknown actor. Imagine trying to persuade somebody to do something without knowing those particulars. By learning to write their Narratio, your students will solve both of those problems and become more persuasive. After all, an informed audience is more readily persuaded and a speaker who knows the facts is much more convincing.

Furthermore, LTW lays foundations for every kind of writing. By cultivating the narrative sense, the ability to link a sequence of causes into a story, this lesson prepares students for short stories, fable-writing, and other forms of creative writing. Consequently, it is an advanced reading lesson, as well.

Your Students Will Learn To:

- ✓ Describe the situation in which the Issue arises
- ✓ Discover the causes of the situation
- ✓ Outline a brief Narratio for the essay

Steps to Teach This Lesson

☐ Begin this class by asking, rather absurdly, "Should he do it?" Wait for a moment and let them start asking questions like, "do what?" "who?" These questions demand a context.

Answer your students' questions, and then ask again, "Should he do it?" Drive them to keep asking more questions to clarify the Issue and the situation. If they slow down, ask them if they know enough and give them additional questions drawn from the definitions this lesson applies:

What can you tell me about the situation?
Who is in this situation?
Where is the actor?
When is the actor making this decision?
What decision does he need to make?
How did he get in this situation?

☐ **Model** the process of forming the Narratio:

Draw on a previous issue from your class discussions, or the examples provided here. The Audience will understand an issue better when they understand the Narratio that goes with it. Students will be able to develop a Narratio more easily if they know the story surrounding the issue.

❖ ***Write your thesis***

❖ Describe the situation in which the actor finds himself:

- *Time*
- *Place*
- *Actors* (usually found right in your Issue)

❖ What action or decision led to this situation?

If your students need guidance in selecting the action or decision that led to this situation, ask them to consider the dilemma. Often this will be a restatement of the issue, but by considering from the actor's perspective- picking a cause that led to this dilemma or need for a decision-they can consider this with a bit more focus on the actor.

❖ What caused the action above? List a sequence of actions, events, and/or decisions that caused the situation.

Notice that your students think "backward" in time from the situation as they identify its causes.

❖ Select the causes to include in your Narratio.

- o When first teaching students to write the Narratio, focus on Relation and establishing a series of causes for this situation.

- o With time, students will be able to consider several types of causes:

    - o Essential causes, without which the situation doesn't make sense
    - o Supporting causes that help show why you adopted the Thesis you chose to defend
    - o Illuminating causes that reveal character and motivation.

Students should be encouraged to judge for themselves what to include in their Narratio. Note, however, that since the Narratio is only a part of the essay and must be presented in due proportion, students do not retell the entire story. They choose the most important causes of the situation (those that are essential, supportive, and illuminating). The Narratio should be shorter than the Proof.

Example:

>**Thesis:** *Edmund should have followed the White Witch.*
>
>**What is the situation of the issue?**
>*Time: Winter in Narnia, World War 2 in England*
>*Place: Narnia, at the sleigh*
>Actors: *Edmund, White Witch*
>Dilemma: *Edmund wants what the White Witch has to offer.*
>
>**What action or event caused this situation?**
>- *The Queen of Narnia approached him in the forest of Narnia.*
>
>**What caused the action above? List a sequence of causes that led to this situation.**
>- *he got lost in the cold,*
>- *he entered the new land of Narnia,*
>- *he was playing hide and seek with his siblings in the Professor's house*
>
>**Decide what to include in the Narratio and order the events.**
>
>- *Situation- Narnia, winter, Edmund*
>- *Meets stranger riding in sled*
>- *Got lost and hungry in the cold*
>- *Entered the land of Narnia through the wardrobe*

Note:
The Narratio is developed after the ANI has been sorted, and your students have already decided their thesis. This will influence the details they include in the Narratio. For example, if they argue that Edmund should not follow the White Witch, they might describe her evil characteristics. If they argue that he should, they might include details about Edmund's lost, cold, and hungry condition.

Show students the proper placement of the Narratio in the Persuasive Essay Template.

I. Introduction
    A. Exordium *
      B. Narratio*
        1. Situation*
        2. Actions*

☐ **Form** several Narratios with your students, using examples provided below, and/or issues from previous essays or class discussions. The more familiar your students are with the story that surrounds their Issues, the more easily they will be able to build a Narratio.

☐ **Review** this lesson by asking your students several questions.

When creating each Narratio, what did we do first?
How did we clarify each situation?
What did we include in each situation?
Then what did we list each time?
How does the Narratio help our audience?
Where do we put the Narratio in the Essay Template?
What is the Narratio?

☐ **Assign** the *Essay Seven Arrangement: Narratio* Worksheet (page 81 in the Student Workbook). Students will also complete the Essay Seven Arrangement Worksheet (page 82) and the Essay Seven Arrangement Template (page 86).

Examples

> **Example A**
> *from "The Gift of the Magi"*

❖ **Thesis:** *Della should cut her hair*

❖ **What is the situation of the issue?**
  Time: Christmas season, possibly Christmas Eve.
  Place: Della's apartment
  Actors: Della and Jim
  Dilemma: Della wants to buy Jim a new watch chain.

- ❖ **What action or event caused this situation?**
  - *Della counts her money and realizes she does not have enough for a gift.*

- ❖ **What caused the action above? List a sequence of causes that led to this situation.**
  - *Della and Jim are poor.*
  - *Jim's salary was recently reduced.*
  - *He doesn't have a chain.*

- ❖ **Decide what to include in the Narratio and order the events:**
  - *Situation: Della's apartment, Christmas time (with Jim and Della), wants to buy a watch chain*
  - *Christmas gift of new chain*
  - *No proper watch chain*
  - *Jim and Della poor*
  - *Jim's salary reduced*

Example B
from To Kill a Mockingbird

- ❖ **Thesis:** *Atticus should defend Tom Robinson.*

- ❖ **What is the situation of the issue?**
  Time: 1930's
  Place: Maycomb, Alabama
  Actors: Tom, Atticus
  Dilemma: Atticus knows that his reputation is at risk if he defends Tom.

- ❖ **What action or event cause the situation?**
  - *The town made it clear they did not like the idea of Atticus defending Tom.*

- ❖ **What caused the action above? List a sequence of causes that led to this situation.**
  The court appointed Atticus as Tom's attorney,

- *Tom Robinson – a black man in the South – was accused of raping a white girl.*

❖ **Decide what to include in the Narratio and order the events:**

- *Situation: Maycomb, Alabama 1930s*

- *Opinion of town unfavorable toward the Finches*

- *Court appoints Atticus as Tom's attorney*

- *Tom Robinson, black man accused of raping a white girl, Mayella Ewell*

Assessment
Confirm that students have:

- ✓ Completed the Narratio Worksheet for their current essay
- ✓ Completed the Essay Seven Arrangement Worksheet
- ✓ Transcribed the Arrangement Seven Template for their current essay

SAMPLE STUDENT WORKSHEET

Essay Seven Arrangement A
A GUIDE TO NARRATIO

Write your Thesis.
_____

Describe the situation in which the actor finds himself:

- *Time*
  _____

- *Place*
  _____

- *Actors*
  _____

What action or decision led to this situation?
_____

What caused the action or decision above? List a sequence of actions, events, and/or decisions
that caused the situation.
_____
_____
_____
_____

Select the causes to include in your Narratio.
_____
_____

Essay Seven Arrangement Template
COMPLETE PERSUASIVE ESSAY

Transcribe your outline onto a separate page, using the template provided below. Replace lines that have an asterisk with your information from the Arrangement Worksheet on the previous pages.

I. Introduction
    A. Exordium*
    B. Narratio
        1. Situation*
        2. Actions*
    C. Division
        1. Agreement*
        2. Disagreement
            a. Thesis*
            b. Counter-Thesis*
    D. Distribution
        1. Thesis*
        2. Enumeration*
        3. Exposition
            a. Proof I*
            b. Proof II*
            c. Proof III*

II. Proof
    A. Proof I*
        1. Sub-proof 1*
        2. Sub-proof 2*
        3. Sub-proof 3*
    B. Proof II*
        1. Sub-proof 1*
        2. Sub-proof 2*
        3. Sub-proof 3*
    C. Proof III*
        1. Sub-proof 1*
        2. Sub-proof 2*
        3. Sub-proof 3*

III. Refutation
    A. Counter-Thesis*
    B. Counter-Proof 1*
        1. Summary of support for reason 1 *
        2. Inadequacy of reason 1*
    C. Counter-Proof 2*
        1. Summary of support for reason 2 *
        2. Inadequacy of reason 2*
    D. Summary of Refutation*

IV. Conclusion
    A. Thesis*
    B. Summary of Proof
        1. Proof I*
        2. Proof II*
        3. Proof III*
    C. Amplification
        1. To whom it matters*
        2. Why it matters to that person or group*

Essay Seven Elocution
ALLITERATION

Tools for the Teacher

Essay Seven Elocution Worksheet (page 87 in the Student Workbook)
Samples from this lesson guide for class discussion

Definitions

- ❖ **Alliteration:** The repetition of adjacent or closely connected consonant sounds
- ❖ **Scheme:** A figure of speech that appeals primarily to the senses

Background for the Teacher

- ❖ **Idea:** Alliteration is a scheme using the repetition of adjacent or closely connected consonant sounds.

- ❖ It can be used to emphasize or highlight an idea, or for just plain fun. This lesson is light-hearted and should be treated accordingly, but it lays foundations for later, more complicated or subtle, schemes.

  Note: Students should incorporate all of the previous tools learned from each Canon in this essay.

Your Students Will Learn to:

- ✓ Describe alliteration
- ✓ Generate series, phrases, or clauses that include alliteration
- ✓ Add alliteration to their essays

Steps to Teach This Lesson

☐ **Begin** by reviewing parallelism. What is it? What is its purpose? How do we create it? What else could be made parallel besides words, phrases, and clauses? Have you ever heard of alliteration?

☐ **Show** students several examples of alliteration. Read the Peter Piper example below (or any tongue twister students may know) several times. What is the same in that verse? Have the students read additional examples of alliteration aloud so they can hear the repeated sounds in several examples.

☐ After students are able to identify alliteration, **show** them how to generate it on their own. You might create a tongue twister with your students, suggesting a consonant sound or blend, then brainstorming words that begin with that sound or blend, and finally creating a tongue twister with those words. Note, however, that tongue twisting does not tax all the advantages of Alliteration.

☐ Next, show them how to apply alliteration to a previous or practice essay.

- Select a seed-word for your alliteration (i.e. a word to start with, from which you will "grow" the scheme in the following steps).

- Identify the consonant sound to repeat.

- Generate additional words that begin with or contain the same consonant sound. It is best to generate words that might fit the sentence, but at this point you are more concerned with simply generating words than you are with selecting them.

    - Encourage students to list more than they think they need to allow for selection in the next step.

- Rewrite the sentence using words from your list.

    - Example: *Aeneas sailed from Troy with a heavy heart.*
    - With alliteration: *Standing silently, Aeneas sailed sadly from Troy.*
    - Keep trying various words and combinations until they easily "roll off" your tongue. A thesaurus or dictionary often proves helpful and should be permitted, but not used as a first option.

> **Example 1**
>
> Select a seed-word for your alliteration:
> *"Caused" from "Edmund caused suffering in Narnia."*
>
> Identify the consonant sound you wish to repeat:
> *"C"*
>
> Generate additional words with the same consonant sound:
> *Careless, crazy, copious, careful, killing, casualties, catastrophe, considerable, calamity*
>
> Rewrite the sentence using as many words as you can from your list:
> *Edmund caused considerable catastrophe for his siblings and all of Narnia.*

> **Example 2**
>
> Select a seed-word for your alliteration:
> *"Sailed" from "Aeneas sailed from Troy with a heavy heart"*
>
> Identify the consonant sound you wish to repeat:
> *"S"*
>
> Generate additional words with the same consonant sound:
> *Silent, sweet, sincere, social, semester, secret, sometimes, sad, stand*
>
> Rewrite the sentence using as many words as you can from your list:
> *Standing silently, Aeneas sailed sadly from Troy.*

☐ **Review** how to identify and generate alliteration. Ask questions like:

- What was the first step you took to generate your first alliteration?
- What did you identify after selecting a word?
- Continue to review each step.
- How will you generate alliteration for your essay?

☐ **Assign** the *Essay Seven Elocution: Alliteration* Worksheet (page 87 in the Student Workbook). Students will add one or more examples of alliteration to their essays.

Remind students to refer to the Essay Seven checklist to confirm that they have completed their essays.

Examples

- From *Peter Piper* (nursery rhyme):

    ***P**eter **P**iper **p**icked a **p**eck of **p**ickled **p**eppers;*
    *A **p**eck of **p**ickled **p**eppers **P**eter **P**iper **p**icked.*
    *If **P**eter **P**iper **p**icked a **p**eck of **p**ickled **p**eppers,*
    *Where's the **p**eck of **p**ickled **p**eppers **P**eter **P**iper **p**icked?*

- From Henry Wadsworth Longfellow's "Paul Revere's Ride":

    *Where the river widens to meet the **b**ay,*
    *A line of **b**lack that **b**ends and floats*
    *On the rising tide like a **b**ridge of **b**oats.*

- From Samuel Taylor Coleridge's "The Rime of the Ancient Mariner":

    *For the **s**ky and the **s**ea,*
    *and the **s**ea and the **s**ky*

- From John F. Kennedy's *Inaugural Address*:

    *With a good conscience our only sure reward, with history the final judge of our deeds, **l**et us go forth to **l**ead the **l**and we **l**ove, asking His blessing and His help, but knowing that here on earth God's work must truly be our own.*

- From *Beowulf*:

    *Hot-hearted **B**eowulf was **b**ent upon **b**attle*

- From Alfred Tennyson's "Sir Galahad":

    ***F**ly o'er waste **f**ens and windy **f**ields*

❖ From Robert Frost's "The Death of the Hired Man":

Mary sat musing on the lamp-flame at the table
***W**aiting for **W**arren.* ***W**hen she heard his step ...*

Assessment
Confirm that students have:

- ✓ Completed Essay Seven Elocution: Alliteration Worksheet
- ✓ Added alliteration to their current essay
- ✓ Written Essay Seven, following the Essay Seven checklist

<u>*Tip:*</u>

Remember, as with any of the schemes or tropes, your students' use of alliteration may initially seem forced. However, through consistent practice, they will improve and hone their skills. At this point, if they can identify and generate alliteration, you have succeeded with this lesson. Captivating writing will follow.

SAMPLE STUDENT WORKSHEET

Essay Seven Elocution
ALLITERATION

Definition

Alliteration is a scheme that uses the repetition of adjacent or closely connected **consonant** sounds.

Examples

From Peter Piper

"**P**eter **P**iper **p**icked a **p**eck of **p**ickled **p**eppers;
A **p**eck of **p**ickled **p**eppers **P**eter **P**iper **p**icked.
If **P**eter **P**iper **p**icked a **p**eck of **p**ickled **p**eppers,
Where's the **p**eck of **p**ickled **p**eppers **P**eter **P**iper **p**icked?"

From Henry Wadsworth Longfellow's *Paul Revere's Ride*

"Where the river widens to meet the **b**ay,--
A line of **b**lack that **b**ends and floats
On the rising tide like a **b**ridge of **b**oats."

From Samuel Taylor Coleridge's *The Rime of the Ancient Mariner*

"For the **s**ky and the **s**ea,
and the **s**ea and the **s**ky . . ."

From John F. Kennedy's Inaugural Address

"With a good conscience our only sure reward, with history the final judge of our deeds, let us go forth to **l**ead the **l**and we **l**ove, asking His blessing and His help, but knowing that here on earth God's work must truly be our own."

From *Beowulf*

"Hot hearted **B**eowulf was **b**ent upon **b**attle."

From Alfred Lord Tennyson's *Sir Galahad*

"Fly o'er **w**aste fens and **w**indy fields."

From Robert Frost's "The Death of a Hired Man"

"Mary sat musing on the lamp-flame at the table
Waiting for **W**arren. **W**hen she heard his
step..."

Steps to Writing Alliteration

1. Select a seed-word to use in your alliteration.
2. Identify the consonant sound to repeat.
3. Generate more words that begin with the same consonant sound and fit your sentence.
4. Rewrite the sentence using words from your list.

Student Examples

> Standing silently, Aeneas sailed sadly away from Troy.

> Longing for a mission, Edmund mindlessly followed the mean tyrant of Narnia.

> Edmund caused careless calamity for his siblings and for all of Narnia.

Practice

1. Use alliteration in a sentence about someone you know, such a family member or friend.

   _____

   _____

2. Use alliteration in a sentence about something you can see outside.

   _____

   _____

3. Use alliteration in a sentence about a character in a favorite book.

_____

_____

**Now add your own examples
of alliteration to Essay Seven.**

ESSAY EIGHT

Essay Eight Invention
TESTIMONY

Tools for the Teacher

Essay Eight Invention Worksheet (page 93 in the Student Workbook)
Samples from this lesson guide for class discussion

Definitions

- **Testimony:** One of the Five Common Topics, **Testimony** asks witnesses to describe either what they saw the actor do in the situation or the character of an actor over time.

- **Eyewitness:** An **eyewitness** is someone who observed the action or situation with which the issue is concerned.

- **Character Witness:** A **character witness** has observed an actor from this situation but in a different situation or situations. He testifies to the person's character, not to the specific action with which the issue is concerned.

Background for the Teacher

- **Idea:** We use Testimony to gather information about the situation and its issue. This lesson explores how to use two kinds of Testimony: eyewitnesses and character witnesses.

- You know Testimony is very useful in court cases, so take advantage of that fact, but don't limit its use to judicial concerns. As you will see below, we frequently use Testimony in our personal lives without being aware of it. LTW prepares students for a great deal more than the Persuasive Essay.

- The first time you teach Testimony, you should apply it to a situation or event that was clearly seen, preferably by multiple witnesses.

- As always, this topic generates information more readily for some issues than others. Rare is the issue, however, that will not benefit from the testimony of witnesses.

- Remember that the Invention lessons always start a new essay, and the skills from previous lessons are repeated for each new essay. Students generate a new issue and start a new ANI.

Your Students Will Learn to:

- ✓ Identify an eyewitness and a character witness
- ✓ Determine what the witness can tell us about the person or the action in the issue
- ✓ Use this information in their ANI

Steps to Teach This Lesson

☐ **Discuss** a time when your students relied on the testimony of someone else to make a decision or judgment. Have they ever asked someone else if they have used a product before buying it for themselves? Have they looked up the review of a book or movie to read what someone else has to say about it? Have they ever taken the report of a friend into account when deciding whether to go somewhere new? Have they ever argued about who was the best ever quarterback, soccer player, skier, etc?

People who make decisions or judgments – like the audience of the essay, actors in the issues, juries, judges, etc. often rely on testimony, as well.

☐ **Model** and present several examples that show how to gather information using the Topic of Testimony. Examples are provided below. Develop some from your class discussions and readings, as well.

> **Teaching Tip**
>
> Use the examples provided here. You have plenty of past issues that you should use as well. Go back to one or two previous essays and show how the Topic of Testimony can be used to gather even more information than your students already had.

After you collect information from a witness, you need to decide how believable that information is. Sometimes witnesses are clearly reliable; other times they aren't. But judging the reliability of a witness can be a tricky and involved process; so to begin, simply show your students that they need to decide. They'll improve through practice.

As this is Invention, encourage your students to wander widely to gather information about their Issues and situation. These tools should give them confidence to explore purposefully rather than worry about rule keeping and checklists.

- ❖ **Describe the situation of the Issue:** Edmund is in the woods and must decide if he will follow the White Witch

- ❖ **Witness #1: Eyewitness**

  - Name an eyewitness
    - *The dwarf*

  - What has this witness seen the actor do or experience in this situation?
    - The White Witch's reaction when she saw Edmund
    - Edmund's reaction to the White Witch
    - The relationship developing between them, based on Edmund's love of Turkish delight

  - How reliable do you consider this witness?

    - Mostly Reliable or Mostly Unreliable

  - Repeat with any additional eyewitnesses

- ❖ **Witness #2: Character Witness**

  - Name a person who knows something about the character of an actor(s) in this situation.
    - *Tumnus the faun knows the White Witch*
  - About whose character can he testify? *White Witch*

  - What did the witness observe and in what circumstances did he observe it?
    - *He has seen the White Witch bring never-ending winter to Narnia,*
    - *He has seen her turn Narnians to stone.*

  - What does that suggest about the character of the actor?
    - *Tumnus knows that she is evil*

- How do these observations relate to the situation?
  - *Tumnus can testify that the White Witch is plotting evil for Edmund and his siblings.*

- How reliable do you consider the witness?

☐ Next, **show** the students how they can use information from a witness and move it to a column in the ANI. Move any appropriate support to the A and N columns.

☐ **Review** The Topic of Testimony with your students.
What kinds of things can a witness tell you about?
What is an eyewitness?
What is a character witness?
What question did you ask the eyewitness each time?
What questions did you ask the character witness each time?
How are these witnesses similar?
How are they different?
How will you apply the Topic of Testimony to gather information for your next essay (or for any decision you need to make)?

☐ **Assign** the Essay Eight Invention: Testimony Worksheet (page 93 in the Student Workbook).

Examples

> **Example A**
> *from "The Gift of the Magi"*

- ❖ **Describe the situation of the Issue:** *Della needs money for Christmas and must decide if she will cut and sell her hair.*

- ❖ **Eyewitness**

  - Name an eyewitness.

    Mne. Sofronie

- What has this witness seen the actor do or experience in this situation?

  She is the one who affirmed that she would buy Della's hair

- How reliable do you consider this witness?

  Reliable

❖ **Character Witness**

- Name a person who knows something about the character of an actor(s) in this situation.

  The Grocer

- About whose character can he testify?

  Della

- What did the witness observe and in what circumstances did he observe it?

  He has seen Della bargaining for cheaper groceries.

- What does that suggest about the character of the actor?

  There is strong evidence that Della has been trying to save money; she knows that they have very limited resources.

- How do these observations relate to the situation?

  With the testimony of the grocer, we know that Della has been trying to save money. Even with this penny-pinching, she still doesn't have enough for Christmas presents.

- How reliable do you consider the witness?

> **Example B**
> *from* The Iliad *by Homer*

- ❖ **Describe the situation of the issue:** *Achilleus, now in his tent, must decide if he will rejoin the fighting.*

- ❖ **Eyewitnesses**

  - Name an eyewitness:

    Patroklos

  - What has this witness seen the actor do or experience in this situation?

    Has seen Achilleus sitting out of the battle
    Saw Achilleus reject the embassy

  - How reliable do you consider this witness?

    Reliable

- ❖ **Character Witness**

  - Name a person who knows something about the character of an actor.

    Nestor

  - About whose character can he testify?

    Achilleus

  - What did the witness observe and in what circumstances did he observe it?

    He has seen him sack cities
    Make offerings to the gods
    Distribute booty among the Greeks
    Submit his winnings to Agamemnon

  - What does that suggest about the character of the actor?

    He knows that he is a great warrior who has, until recently, accepted the hierarchy and traditions of army life.

- How do these observations relate to the situation?

  Nestor has great confidence that Achilleus' honor will compel him back into battle.

- Is the witness reliable?

  Yes

Assessment
Confirm that students have:

- ✓ Completed the Essay Eight Invention: Testimony Worksheet for the current essay
- ✓ Have moved any relevant points from the Testimony Worksheet to their ANI charts

SAMPLE STUDENT WORKSHEET

Essay Eight Invention
TESTIMONY

There are two kinds of testimony you will consider in this exercise: the eyewitness and the character witness.

- An **eye witness** is someone who observed the action or situation with which the Issue is concerned.

- A **character witness** has observed a person who is involved in the situation. The character witness has observed this person in a different situation and bears witness to his character.

The witness will bear witness to the actor and actions; the witness is not a judge.

Describe the situation of the Issue.
_____

Witness #1: Eyewitness

1. Name an eyewitness.
_____

2. What has this witness seen the actor do or experience in this situation?
_____
_____

3. How reliable do you consider this witness? Check one.

☐ Mostly Reliable

☐ Mostly Unreliable

4. Name an additional eyewitness.
_____
_____

5. What has this witness seen?
_____
_____

6. How reliable do you consider this witness? Check one.

☐ Mostly Reliable

☐ Mostly Unreliable

7. Repeat with any additional eyewitnesses.

Witness #2: Character Witness

1. Write the name of a person who knows something about the character of an actor(s) in this situation.
_____

2. About whose character can he testify?
_____
_____

3. What did the witness observe and in what circumstances did he observe it?
_____
_____

4. What does that suggest about the character of the actor?

_____

_____

5. How do these observations relate to the situation?

_____

_____

6. How reliable do you consider the witness? Check one.

    ❏ Mostly unreliable
    ❏ Mostly reliable

**Review your I column, and move any
appropriate items to the A or N columns.**

Lesson 8 Arrangement Review
COMPLETE PERSUASIVE ESSAY OUTLINE

You now have time to review (and diagnose weaknesses in) all of the Arrangement parts taught in LTW Level 1.

- *The last lessons taught have had the least review. Your students might benefit from extra discussion and practice with the Narratio and/or Refutation as they have only written one or two of these on their own.*

- *Your students should be confident in understanding and using the first tools taught in Level 1 by now. They have had several essays to practice Exordium and Amplification, so this might be the time to challenge them a bit. Can they give greater consideration to their audience?*

- *To assess your students' retention of the rhetoric terms taught this year, a short quiz on Arrangement terms can be appropriate.*

- *You can assess your students' understanding of the ideas of Arrangement by asking them to identify examples of each in sample essays.*

- *You can also assess their understanding of the Complete Persuasive Essay Template by asking them to write out a Template from memory.*

Homework: Students demonstrate the Order of Development by writing out the parts of a Complete Persuasive Essay. By now, students have internalized the worksheet and can write this information in the correct order from memory and habit. Then students demonstrate the Order of Writing by transcribing a Complete Persuasive Essay Template without a guide.

Essay Eight Elocution
METAPHOR

Tools for the Teacher

Essay Eight Elocution Worksheet (page 96 in the Student Workbook)
Samples from this lesson guide for class discussion

Definitions

- ❖ **Metaphor:** A rhetorical trope in which an indirect comparison is made of two different kinds of things.

- ❖ **Trope:** A figure of speech that appeals to the imagination (whereas a scheme appeals to the senses).

Background for the Teacher

- ❖ **Idea:** Metaphor is a rhetorical trope that indirectly compares two things that are different in kind but that share a common characteristic.

    Note that metaphor is related to a simile, but omits the words "like" and "as" or any other words that make the comparison explicit.

    Metaphors can be developed for people, actions, and objects, but they are particularly helpful when you want to explore or express feelings and abstract ideas.

    Every trope depends on some sort of comparison, so similes and metaphors prepare students to learn a practically unlimited number of figures of speech. This is one way that LTW prepares students to write poetry, even while practicing persuasive essays.

Your Students Will Learn To:

- ✓ Describe a metaphor
- ✓ Generate their own metaphors
- ✓ Add metaphors to their essays

Steps to Teach This Lesson

☐ **Review** similes by generating new examples or asking several students to share similes from their essays or things they have read. Ask them to describe simile and how to develop a simile.

Transition to metaphors by asking them to read several similes without the comparative words, usually "like" or "as."

☐ **Present** examples of literary metaphors, including those provided below. You can find many more in books, article, on-line or even in common speech. Ask your students what these metaphors have in common, how they are like similes, and how they are different. Once they can identify metaphors, add some simple comparisons as well, so they see that not every indirect comparison is a metaphor. "AnnaClaire is a Southern Belle" is not a metaphor.

Clichés are often lazy metaphors, couch potatoes that won't think for themselves.

☐ **Next, teach** your students how to generate their own metaphors. The verbs "is" "has" and "does" can help generate metaphors just as they helped generate comparisons and similes earlier.

Model the steps to writing a metaphor with your students as many times as necessary.

Steps:

- Select a person, thing, or idea that you will develop with a metaphor. *e.g. friendship*

- Identify a trait or action of the item selected. *e.g. warmth*

- Identify a thing of a different kind that possesses or seems to possess the same trait or is marked by the same action(the more concrete and different from the first thing, the better). *e.g. blanket*

- Combine the two things, stating that one thing is the other thing.
  Friendship is a warm blanket.

> ### Example 1
>
> Select an item you will develop with a metaphor:
> *Mr. and Mrs. Beaver*
>
> Identify a trait or action found in that thing:
> *offer security to the Pevensies*
>
> Identify a thing of a different kind that possesses the same trait or action:
> *A fortress*
>
> Combine the two things, stating that one thing is the other thing. Make any necessary changes to maintain the unity of the sentence.
> *Mr. and Mrs. Beaver are a fortress for the Pevensies.*

> ### Example 2
>
> Select an idea you will develop with a metaphor:
> *Education*
>
> Identify a trait or action possessed by that idea:
> *Fruitful*
>
> Identify a thing of a different kind that manifests the same trait or action:
> *A garden*
>
> Combine the two things, stating that one thing is the other thing. Make any necessary changes to maintain the unity of the sentence.
> *Education is a garden.*

Note: Sometimes it is easier to generate a metaphor for an idea if you reverse the order and come up with a picture for the idea first and then ask why that picture came to mind. Much of the value of the metaphor is in the way it helps you realize things you wouldn't have realized without it.

> **Example 3**
>
> Select an activity you will develop with a metaphor:
> *reading*
>
> Identify a trait or action found in that thing:
> *exploration*
>
> Identify a thing of a different kind that manifests the same trait or action:
> *journey*
>
> Rewrite the sentence by saying the first thing is the second one.
> Make any necessary changes to maintain the unity of the sentence.
> *Reading is a journey to a foreign land.*

☐ **Ask** the students to compare, and then to explain, the steps you took to create each metaphor.

- *What steps did you take to create a metaphor?*
- *How did you start?*
- *What did you identify about that thing each time?*

☐ **Assign** the *Essay Eight Elocution: Metaphor* Worksheet (page 96 in the Student Workbook).

☐ **Assign** students to use metaphor in their essay this week.

Examples

❖ *From Shakespeare's* Sonnet 147:

My reason, the physician to my love,
Angry that his prescriptions are not kept,
Hath left me

❖ *From Samuel Taylor Coleridge's* Pain:

I too could laugh and play...

Ere Tyrant Pain had chased away delight

- ❖ *From Robert Louis Stevenson:*

    A friend is a gift you give yourself

- ❖ *From Robert Louis Stevenson:*

    Everyone, at some time or another, sits down to a banquet of consequences.

- ❖ *From Groucho Marx:*

    A hospital bed is a parked taxi with the meter running.

Assessment
Confirm that students have:

- ✓ Completed Essay Eight Elocution: Metaphor Worksheet
- ✓ Added metaphor to their current essay
- ✓ Written Essay Eight, following the Essay Eight checklist

Their first attempts inventing metaphor might sound wooden, but as your students practice they will refine their skills and learn to express more and more impressive metaphors. Encourage them to look for metaphors in the things they read.

SAMPLE STUDENT WORKSHEET

Essay Eight Elocution
METAPHOR

Definition

Metaphor, a trope, is an indirect comparison of two different kinds of things (indirect- i.e., you do not use "like" or "as").

Examples

From Shakespeare's *A Comedy of Errors*

"A man may break a word with you, sir, and words are but wind."

From John 15:5

"I am the vine, ye are the branches . . ."

From Psalm 23:1

"The Lord is my shepherd . . ."

From John Donne

"Reason is our soul's left hand, faith her right."

From Psalm 5:9

"Their throat is an open sepulcher; with their tongues they have used deceit."

From William Shakespeare's Sonnet 147

"My reason, the physician to my love,
Angry that his prescriptions are not kept,
Hath left me. .."

Steps to Creating a Metaphor

a) Select a thing that you will develop with a metaphor.
b) Identify a trait or action of the thing selected.
c) Identify a thing of a different kind that possesses or seems to possess the same trait or is marked by the same action(the more concrete and different from the first thing, the better).
d) Combine the two things, stating that one thing is the other.

Student Examples

My books are my airplanes.

That phone is a flock of birds.

Practice

Write a metaphor about someone you know, such as a family member or a friend.

Identify someone to write a metaphor about.
_____

Identify a trait or action displayed by that person.
_____
_____

Identify a thing of a different kind that shares that trait or action.
_____

Completed Metaphor:
_____
_____
_____

Write a metaphor about something you can see or imagine.

Identify something to write a metaphor about.
_____

Identify a trait or action displayed by that thing.
_____
_____

Identify a thing of a different kind that shares that trait or action.

_____

Completed Metaphor:

_____
_____
_____

Write a metaphor about a character in a favorite book.

Identify a character to write a metaphor about.

_____

Identify a trait or action displayed by that character.

_____
_____

Identify a different character that shares that trait or action.

_____

Completed Metaphor:

_____
_____
_____

**Now add your own examples of
metaphor to Essay Eight.**

ESSAY NINE

Lesson 9 Invention Review
FIVE COMMON TOPICS

In class, return to the Essay Two Invention: Five Common Topics worksheet. Your students will quickly see how much they now know about these five topics, and they should be able to use the topics quite effectively.

This worksheet can now serve as a review guide and a prompt for students to apply the specific generative tools they have learned over the past year.

To review the Five Common Topics, ask students to use all five topics to generate information on a new issue. You can use an issue from your current studies and allow students to work together in class, generating as much information as they can during the class time. This review, practice, and class interaction will help solidify these Invention ideas in their minds.

Homework: Students start a new issue and complete a full set of Invention work outside of class.

Lesson 9 Arrangement
FINAL REVIEW

You are done! You have recovered a year's worth of *The Lost Tools of Writing*™. You have laid the foundation for every kind of writing and speaking you and your students will ever encounter, including essay writing, storytelling, poetry, debate, and speech.

If you have time for extra review or writing activities, here are some suggestions:

- The 20-minute essay workout
- Mad Group poem
- Just a Minute
- Storytelling games
- Spontaneous debate
- Impromptu speech

The 20-minute essay can be a mentally challenging game, and it prepares students for the new SAT essay as well. Give your students an issue or question and 20 minutes to write about it. After 20 minutes tell them to stop and exchange the essay with a classmate.

Here you have two options. You can either have the classmate evaluate the essay for the parts of an essay or you can have the classmate complete and edit the first student's essay for 20 minutes. This might involve adding schemes and tropes, Narratio, or a Refutation. The point is to do it in a playful, lighthearted way.

A **Mad Group poem** draws the class together in the process of writing a poem. Every student writes a simple descriptive sentence, then hands his statement to the student beside him. The next student adds a simile. The next adds a scheme. You continue going on adding schemes and tropes until at last you have a very unwieldy poem, with schemes and tropes crowding it like weeds. At this point you can either enjoy the silliness of the poem, or you can assign one student to reformat each poem into a rhyme scheme and/or meter.

Just a Minute is a game played aloud. You will need a stopwatch. One student is given a subject and has one minute to talk about it. She must do so without repeating herself, hesitating, or stumbling. If she does, a classmate can call her on it. The second classmate now has the opportunity to finish the minute on the same topic but any classmate can call him if he repeats, hesitates, or stumbles. Five points are awarded to any player who can speak for an entire minute without being called. Two points are awarded to the player who finishes the minute without having begun it.

Any subject suits this game as it always challenges the imagination of the players. Detergent, vitamin B, asphalt, and swimming pools can be just as much fun as the stars, cars, football, and music.

You and your students can choose from many **storytelling games**. At CiRCE we like to play what we call "The Canterbury Club." The basic idea is that four people play, going around in turns. First time around, each player names or makes up a character. The second time, each player names a setting. The third time, the first player chooses one of the four characters as the protagonist, the second chooses the antagonist, and the third chooses the sidekick to the protagonist. The fourth then states the problem the protagonist has to solve. From there you can expect a good bout of madness. Continue around the circle, giving each storyteller one minute to develop his part of the story.

A **spontaneous debate** is not for the faint of heart. An Issue is presented, sides are formed, and no more than ten minutes later the two sides present their cases following the basic debate format of your choice as a teacher. To simplify, you could use the Persuasive Essay outline as the structure of each side's position.

For an **impromptu speech** you will need a hat. Write on small pieces of paper all the topics your students have learned while mastering the tools of Invention. Then put the papers in a hat. The Five Topics can be broken down into quite a few more. For example, Comparison can be divided into Difference of Degree, Difference of Kind and Similarities. Each student draws one topic from the hat.

A subject or Issue is then assigned for oratory. Each student in the class presents a speech on the subject based on his or her topic. For example, the subject might be Napoleon. One student might offer a speech based on the topic of similarity by showing how Napoleon was similar to three other people. Another might present his insights based on the topic of Circumstance by discussing what was happening in the world at the time of Napoleon.

The activities most directly and obviously related to *The Lost Tools of Writing*™ are the 20-minute essay and the impromptu speech. But the point of this program is to teach students to think both creatively and with discipline. They should have gained a great deal of confidence in all these activities by the end of the first year.

And they have barely scratched the surface of what they will be learning over the next few years!

Essay Nine Elocution
ASSONANCE

Tools for the Teacher

Student Workbook pg. 103
Samples from this lesson guide for class discussion

Definitions

- ❖ **Assonance:** A rhetorical scheme in which a vowel sound is repeated in adjacent or closely connected words.

Background for the Teacher

- ❖ **Idea:** Assonance is a scheme in which a vowel sound is repeated. Your students will learn to identify assonance and to generate assonance. Assonance is much less obtrusive than alliteration.

    In contrast, alliteration is a scheme in which a consonant sound is repeated.

    Note that if the words rhyme, you have a rhyme scheme, not assonance

---

Your Students Will Learn to:

- ✓ Describe assonance
- ✓ Generate series, phrases, or clauses that include Assonance
- ✓ Add assonance to their essays

Steps to Teach Assonance

☐ **Review** alliteration by asking several students to share examples of alliteration from their essays or things they have read and asking them to describe alliteration. Ask if they can think of any other ways to play with sounds.

☐ **Show** several examples of assonance. You can find several examples. Read the first example a few times so they can hear and identify the repeated vowel sound. Ask them to identify the repeated vowel sounds in each example. Note the subtle emphasis that assonance provides, much less than alliteration.

☐ After your students are able to identify assonance, **show** them how to generate it on their own.

- *Select a seed-word whose vowel sound you wish to repeat.*

- *Identify the vowel sound to repeat.*

- *Generate additional words that include the same vowel sound. Encourage your students to generate more than they think they need to allow for selection when they create a new sentence in the next step.*

- *Rewrite the sentence using words from your list. Make necessary changes to keep your sentence coherent.*

Example 1

Select a word whose sound you wish to repeat:
"Stopped" from "Achilleus stopped fighting"

Identify the vowel sound you wish to repeat:
Short "o"

Come up with more words that include the same vowel sound, but have different consonant sounds surrounding that vowel:
Flop, pop, yawn, top, rock, stop, thought, cause

Rewrite the sentence using as many words as you can from your list. (You may think of more as you put them together.) Make any necessary changes to maintain the unity of the sentence:
Achilleus yawned and thought he was their rock and their rod, on top of their applause.

> **Example 2**
>
> Select a word whose sound you wish to repeat:
> *"dream" from "Anne likes to dream"*
>
> Identify the vowel sound you wish to repeat:
> *Long "e"*
>
> Come up with more words that include the same vowel sound, but have different consonant sounds surrounding that vowel:
> *Leave, seem, lead, peace, drink, flee, need, freedom, sweet, seeks*
>
> Rewrite the sentence using as many words as you can from your list. (You may think of more as you put them together.) Make any necessary changes to maintain the unity of the sentence:
> *When Anne dreams, she sees the peace she seeks and needs.*

☐ **Review** how to identify and generate assonance. Compare the steps you took each time. Ask questions like:

- *What was the first step you took to generate assonance?*
- *What did you identify after selecting a word?*
- *How will you generate assonance for your essays?*

Ask them to compare these examples with alliteration.

☐ Assign the Assonance Worksheet in the Student Workbook and direct them to add assonance to their essays.

Examples

- From Edgar Allen Poe's "The Bells":

    *"Hear the mellow wedding bells—
    Golden bells!"*

- From Dylan Thomas's "Battle of the Long-Legged Bait":

*"Wh**a**les in the w**a**ke like c**a**pes and Alps,
Qu**a**ked the sick sea and snouted deep"*

- From Shakespeare's *Romeo and Juliet*:

*"Is cr**i**mson **i**n thy l**i**ps, and **i**n thy cheeks?"*

- Martin Luther King Junior's "I Have a Dream Speech":

*"We m**u**st forever cond**u**ct our str**u**ggle on the high plane of d**i**gn**i**ty and d**i**sc**i**pline."*

- From Robert Louis Stevenson:

*"**I**n our w**i**ld cl**i**mate, **i**n our scowling town...
The belching wh**i**stle w**i**nd, the m**i**ssile rain"*

Assessment
Confirm that students have:

- ✓ Completed Essay Nine Elocution: Assonance Worksheet
- ✓ Added assonance to their current essay
- ✓ Written Essay Nine, and checked it against the Essay Nine checklist

SAMPLE STUDENT WORKSHEET

Essay Nine Elocution
ASSONANCE

Definition

Assonance is a scheme in which one vowel sound is repeated in adjacent or closely connected words.

Examples

From Shelley's Sonnet "England in 1819"

"An old mad, blind, despised, and dying king—
Princes, the dregs of their dull race, who flow
Through public scorn—mud from a muddy spring."

From W.B. Yeats' "Byzantium"

"Those images that yet,
Fresh images beget,
That dolphin-torn, that gong-tormented sea"

From Robert Frost's "After Apple-Picking"

"St**e**m **e**nd and blossom **e**nd,
And every fl**e**ck of russ**e**t showing clear . . ."

From J. R. R. Tolkien's *The Two Towers*

"I make the earth sh**a**ke as I tr**a**mp through the gr**a**ss;
trees cr**a**ck **a**s I p**a**ss."

Steps to Creating Assonance

1. Select a seed-word whose vowel sound you wish to repeat.
2. Identify the vowel sound.
3. Generate more words that include the same vowel sound.
4. Rewrite the sentence using words from your list. Make any necessary changes to be sure your sentence makes sense.

Student Examples

Achilles yawned and thought--he was their rock and their rod, on top of their applause.

If Anne dreams, she sees the peace she seeks and needs.

In time, if he rides, keeps good line, feels bright, hits the side—he can find a sign and do right.

Practice

1. Write a sentence using assonance about someone you know, such as a family member or a friend.

_____

2. Write a sentence using assonance about something you can see outside.

3. Write a sentence using assonance about a character in a favorite book.

**Now add your own examples
of assonance to Essay Nine.**

APPENDIX A
HOW TO EDIT

Next, you will guide your students through the process of self-editing, or revising their essays. Editing is often neglected or hastily done, but is equally as important a step as any other in the writing process.

THE EDITING PROCESS

Before your students turn in their essays for you to assess, they will revise them using the following steps:

- **Read** your first draft. As you read, mark words, phrases, or sentences that might need revision.

- **Revise** your essay by following the *Self-Edit Checklist* for your essay. Work through each checkpoint double-checking that you have included each assigned essay part.

- **Rewrite** your essay with the corrections you have made.

- **Reread** your new draft.

Your students should repeat this process as many times as necessary.

SELF-EDIT CHECKLISTS

A *Self-Edit Checklist* has been written for each essay you will teach in *The Lost Tools of Writing*. You will find the checklists on the following pages as well as in the back of the Student Workbook.

ESSAY 1: RUDIMENTARY PERSUASIVE ESSAY - OUTLINE TO TEXT

- ☐ Essay follows Template 1

- ☐ Introduction has a thesis with enumeration and exposition

- ☐ The first proof begins as "The first reason..." followed by the thesis and proof

- ☐ The second proof begins as "The second reason..." followed by the thesis and proof

- ☐ The third proof begins as "The third reason..." followed by the thesis and proof

- ☐ Conclusion restates the thesis and summarizes the proofs in a single sentence without the enumeration

- ☐ Checked spelling of uncertain words in a dictionary

- ☐ Checked grammar
    - o Verb tense is consistent
    - o Subjects and verbs agree
    - o Repaired fragments and run-ons

- ☐ Checked punctuation
    - o Capital letters are used correctly
    - o Commas, colons, semi-colons, and hyphens are used correctly
    - o Correct end punctuation is used

ESSAY 2: INTRODUCTORY PERSUASIVE ESSAY	ESSAY 3: BASIC PERSUASIVE ESSAY – EXORDIUM
☐ Essay follows Template 2	☐ Essay follows Template 3
☐ Introduction has a thesis with enumeration and exposition	☐ Exordium is added to the beginning of the essay
☐ Main proofs are written clearly	☐ Introduction has a thesis with enumeration and exposition
☐ Each main proof is supported by three sub-proofs	☐ Main proofs are written clearly and supported with sub-proofs
☐ Conclusion restates the thesis and summarizes the proofs in a single sentence without the enumeration	☐ Repaired weak verbs 　o Vague 　o Passive
☐ Marked and labeled scheme 1—Parallelism: words	☐ Marked and labeled scheme 1—Parallelism: words
☐ Checked spelling of uncertain words in a dictionary	☐ Checked spelling of uncertain words in a dictionary
☐ Checked grammar 　o Verb tense is consistent 　o Subjects and verbs agree 　o Repaired fragments and run-ons 　o Checked punctuation 　o Commas, colons, semicolons, and hyphens are used correctly 　o Correct end punctuation is used 　o Capital letters are used	☐ Checked grammar 　o Verb tense is consistent 　o Subjects and verbs agree 　o Repaired fragments and run-ons ☐ Checked punctuation 　o Capital letters are used correctly 　o Commas, colons, semicolons, and hyphens are used correctly 　o Correct end punctuation is used

ESSAY 4: BASIC PERSUASIVE ESSAY – AMPLIFICATION

- ☐ Essay follows Template 4
- ☐ Amplification is added to the end of the essay
- ☐ Main proofs are written clearly and supported with sub-proofs
- ☐ Proofs are parallel
- ☐ Exordium is added to the beginning of the essay
- ☐ Introduction has a thesis with enumeration and exposition
- ☐ Repaired weak verbs
  - o Vague
  - o Passive
- ☐ Marked and labeled each scheme
  - o Parallelism 1: words
  - o Parallelism 2: phrases or clauses
- ☐ Checked spelling of uncertain words in a dictionary
- ☐ Checked grammar
  - o Verb tense is consistent
  - o Subjects and verbs agree
  - o Repaired fragments and run-ons
- ☐ Checked punctuation
  - o Capital letters are used correctly
  - o Commas, colons, semicolons, and hyphens are used correctly
  - o Correct end punctuation is used
  - o Quotation marks are used correctly

ESSAY 5: BASIC PERSUASIVE ESSAY – DIVISION & DISTRIBUTION

- ☐ Essay follows Template 5
- ☐ Division is added to the essay
- ☐ Main proofs are written clearly and supported with sub-proofs
- ☐ Proofs are parallel
- ☐ Amplification is added to the end of the essay
- ☐ Introduction has a thesis with enumeration and exposition
- ☐ Exordium is added to the beginning of the essay
- ☐ Repaired weak verbs
  - o Vague
  - o Passive
- ☐ Marked and labeled each scheme
  - o Parallelism 1 and 2
  - o Antithesis
- ☐ Checked spelling of uncertain words in a dictionary
- ☐ Checked grammar
  - o Verb tense is consistent
  - o Subjects and verbs agree
  - o Repaired fragments and run-ons
- ☐ Checked punctuation
  - o Capital letters are used correctly
  - o Commas, colons, semicolons, and hyphens are used correctly
  - o Correct end punctuation is used
  - o Quotation marks are used correctly

ESSAY 6: BASIC PERSUASIVE ESSAY – REFUTATION	ESSAY 7: COMPLETE PERSUASIVE ESSAY – NARRATIO

☐ Essay follows Template 6
☐ Refutation is added to the essay
☐ Main proofs are written clearly and supported with sub-proofs
☐ Proofs are parallel
☐ Amplification is added to the end of the essay
☐ Introduction has a thesis with enumeration and exposition
☐ Division is added to the essay
☐ Exordium is added to the beginning of the essay
 	
☐ Repaired weak verbs
   ○ Vague
   ○ Passive
☐ Marked and labeled each scheme
   ○ Parallelism 1 and 2
   ○ Antithesis
☐ Marked and labeled each trope
   ○ Simile
☐ Checked spelling of uncertain words in a dictionary
☐ Checked grammar
   ○ Verb tense is consistent
   ○ Subjects and verbs agree
   ○ Repaired fragments and run-ons
☐ Checked punctuation
   ○ Capital letters are used correctly
   ○ Commas, colons, semicolons, and hyphens are used correctly
   ○ Correct end punctuation is used
   ○ Quotation marks are used correctly
	☐ Essay follows Template 7
	☐ Narratio is added to the essay
	☐ Refutation is added to the essay
	☐ Main proofs are written clearly and supported with sub-proofs
	☐ Proofs are parallel
	☐ Amplification is added to the end of the essay
	☐ Introduction has a thesis with enumeration and exposition
	☐ Division is added to the essay
	☐ Exordium is added to the beginning of the essay
	
	☐ Repaired weak verbs
	   ○ Vague
	   ○ Passive
	☐ Marked and labeled each scheme
	   ○ Parallelism 1 and 2
	   ○ Antithesis
	   ○ Alliteration
	☐ Marked and labeled each trope
	   ○ Simile
	☐ Checked spelling of uncertain words in a dictionary
	☐ Checked grammar
	   ○ Verb tense is consistent
	   ○ Subjects and verbs agree
	   ○ Repaired fragments and run-ons
	☐ Checked punctuation
	   ○ Capital letters are used correctly
	   ○ Commas, colons, semicolons, and hyphens are used correctly
	   ○ Correct end punctuation is used
	   ○ Quotation marks are used correctly

ESSAY 8: COMPLETE PERSUASIVE ESSAY – REVIEW & PRACTICE

- ☐ Essay follows Template 8
- ☐ Narratio is added to the essay
- ☐ Refutation is added to the essay
- ☐ Main proofs are written clearly and supported with sub-proofs
- ☐ Proofs are parallel
- ☐ Amplification is added to the end of the essay
- ☐ Introduction has a thesis with enumeration and exposition
- ☐ Division is added to the essay
- ☐ Exordium is added to the beginning of the essay
- ☐ Repaired weak verbs
  - o Vague
  - o Passive
- ☐ Marked and labeled each scheme
  - o Parallelism
  - o Antithesis
  - o Alliteration
- ☐ Marked and labeled each trope
  - o Simile
  - o Metaphor
- ☐ Checked spelling of uncertain words in a dictionary
- ☐ Checked grammar
  - o Verb tense is consistent
  - o Subjects and verbs agree
  - o Repaired fragments and run-ons
- ☐ Checked punctuation
  - o Capital letters are used correctly
  - o Commas, colons, semicolons, and hyphens are used correctly
  - o Correct end punctuation is used
  - o Quotation marks are used correctly

ESSAY 9: COMPLETE PERSUASIVE ESSAY – REVIEW & PRACTICE

- ☐ Essay follows Template 9
- ☐ Narratio is added to the essay
- ☐ Refutation is added to the essay
- ☐ Main proofs are written clearly and supported with sub-proofs
- ☐ Proofs are parallel
- ☐ Amplification is added to the end of the essay
- ☐ Introduction has a thesis with enumeration and exposition
- ☐ Division is added to the essay
- ☐ Exordium is added to the beginning of the essay
- ☐ Repaired weak verbs
  - o Vague
  - o Passive
- ☐ Marked and labeled each scheme
  - o Parallelism
  - o Antithesis
  - o Alliteration
  - o Assonance
- ☐ Marked and labeled each trope
  - o Simile
  - o Metaphor
- ☐ Checked spelling of uncertain words in a dictionary
- ☐ Checked grammar
  - o Verb tense is consistent
  - o Subjects and verbs agree
  - o Repaired fragments and run-ons
- ☐ Checked punctuation
  - o Capital letters are used correctly
  - o Commas, colons, semicolons, and hyphens are used correctly
  - o Correct end punctuation is used
  - o Quotation marks are used correctly

APPENDIX B
A GUIDE TO ASSESSMENT

Appropriate feedback makes writing instruction effective. This section describes how to use assessment to encourage, correct, and guide your students on the road to mastery of writing and, through writing, to wisdom, virtue, and self-governance.

What is assessment and what is it for?

Assessment is the act of evaluating how well your students have learned new skills and ideas by comparing their work to a standard. It is guided by two questions: "With what standard will I compare their work?" and, "How will I communicate the assessment to my students?"

Assessment takes place in three time-perspectives: short, middle, and long-term. The standards for comparison are determined by the perspective from which you are viewing the work.

The short-term perspective is concerned with the immediate lesson. Each lesson has its own objective, so effective assessment directs your students' attention to specific actions that enable them to reach that objective. By providing prompt and objective feedback, you guide your students as they practice specific skills to complete their assignments.

The middle-term perspective is concerned with your students' overall ability to write better. They will reach this more general objective by achieving specific short-term successes, practice by practice, lesson by lesson, building the understanding and skills that make them effective writers.

The long-term perspective is concerned with your students' independence as writers and, ultimately, as people. You will teach your students effective self-assessment by showing them patterns of assessment that they will internalize and use to assess their own writing. By knowing why and how you are assessing, they gain confidence in their ability to assess their own work. In that sense, you are equipping them to become self-governing people through writing.

Thus, by providing effective assessment for the current lesson, you help them write better, and by helping them write better, you equip your students to assess their own work and achieve the priceless gift of independence.

FORMAL AND INFORMAL

Sometimes you will assess their work formally, providing your students feedback in written responses. Far more often, your feedback will be informal, celebrating gains, correcting errors, and encouraging perseverance in response to specific actions and situations.

Formal or informal, feedback must be objective and useful. That is, it must be *appropriate, clear, known*, and *actionable*. Assessment is *appropriate* when it is drawn from the assignment and supports the lesson. It is *clear* when it is well-explained by the teacher and understood by the student. When expectations are communicated ahead of time, they can be *known* by your students, who can work with confidence toward the stated and understood end. For students to respond to feedback, it must be *actionable*. Avoid vague feedback, especially when it is negative. Do not use feedback to express frustration, but to grow together.

3 COLUMNS

When you assess, you will find it helpful to remember the three different kinds of learning. Your students can remember information, understand ideas, and master skills. Each is learned, taught, and assessed differently.

Since it is an art, writing consists of a number of skills, and skills must be coached. In particular, you will coach your students in the process of generating an essay: Invention, Arrangement, and Elocution.

Coaching involves *modeling* by the coach, *imitation* by the writer, *feedback* by the coach, and *responses* by the writer. The *models* the writer *imitates* are provided in the LTW lessons. Here we address feedback and response.

To assess a skill, you (the coach) identify milestones along the path to mastery and then determine whether your students have reached them. Your feedback tells them whether they have reached the milestone and how to reach it if they have not. *The Lost Tools of Writing*™ guides your students from milestone to milestone, so it is natural and relatively easy to use the milestones to assess your students' work.

Each canon contains its own milestones. For example, while learning Invention, your students will compare terms by finding similarities; later, they will find differences in degree: two milestones, rightly ordered.

You will provide feedback to your students at three levels:

- Practice (the exercises undertaken to learn the new skill)
- Performance (the process of writing the essay)
- Product (the essay itself)

ASSESSING PRACTICE

Practice, as any soccer coach or music teacher will remind you, is most important. Performance is second; the product is third. Writers who practice well perform well. When they perform well, they produce good products.

When students practice, they need continuous, immediate, and specific feedback. Avoid looking over their shoulders, but fix mistakes and honor success frequently, kindly, and in small doses, especially when your students are practicing something for the first time and are hungry for feedback.

For example, before they are required to add similes to their essays, they should practice generating similes as an isolated exercise apart from their essays. Tell them immediately whether they did it correctly or how to practice differently.

Be specific about how to alter their practice. If, for example, they generated a simple comparison (e.g. footballs with baseballs) instead of a simile (e.g. Julius Caesar with a wildfire), remind them to identify an object that has a quality similar to the subject (both have destructive power) but is of a different kind than the subject (wildfire is a force of nature, while Julius Caesar is a rational person).

Students are most receptive to criticism when they are practicing. If they don't receive that feedback then, they are much less likely to appreciate it later, when it is too late to use.

This rapid, continuous, specific feedback is best presented informally. It should be prompt and matter of fact. If they practiced correctly, celebrate it. If they erred, enjoy what was right and discover where they went wrong. Either tell them or discuss with them how they could have done it correctly. Then instruct them to *practice again immediately* and give prompt feedback to that exercise until they are able to execute the task correctly.

To provide feedback on Invention practice, informally review their class exercises and the exercise pages with which they practice each topic of invention.

To provide feedback on Arrangement practice, review and respond to their class exercises and to the exercise pages with which they practice the process of adding new elements to the outline.

To provide feedback on Elocution practice, review and respond to their class exercises and to the exercise pages with which they practice the scheme, trope, or editing skill they will add to their essays.

ASSESSING PERFORMANCE

Fine arts, like painting and writing, are different from performance arts, like dancing or playing an instrument. Fine art leaves something behind, while a performance is itself the product of a performance art. When you stop writing, you have an essay. When you stop dancing, you have a memory, but the dance is over.

Furthermore, writing tends to be a private activity, so watching them "perform" can make your students uncomfortable. However, you can approach their performance indirectly by assessing the materials they generate under the canons of Invention, Arrangement, and Elocution.

These canon materials are an intermediate product (the final product is the final essay). They will give you a snapshot of what your students are thinking, capturing them in motion, so to speak. As a result, you can provide feedback that your student can act on.

To assess Invention performance, review and respond to their ANI charts, ensuring that each column has as much information as required.

To assess Arrangement performance, review and respond to their outlines, ensuring that each element of the essay is where it belongs.

To assess Elocution performance, review and respond to their first drafts, ensuring that the new scheme, trope, or editing skill has been added to their essays.

ASSESSING THE PRODUCT

Finally, you will assess your students' final product or artifact: the completed essay. While it is the least important of the three elements, the written essay remains the goal of the Invention, Arrangement, and Elocution exercises. Along the way, you will also assess each Invention and Arrangement product.

To assess the Invention product, confirm that your students have included the required amount of information under each column. Since you will have done this when you assessed their performance, you will simply need to confirm it this time.

To assess the Arrangement product, confirm that their completed outlines still follow the right pattern.

To assess the Elocution product, the essay, ensure that all required elements were correctly included. As you do so, note exercises for review in later teaching sessions to edify any weak areas. Especially note accomplishments that should be honored.

THE CYCLE

As you can see, you assess all three canons (Invention, Arrangement, and Elocution) and within each you will be assessing practice, performance, and product. However, it is not as overwhelming as it may sound. You assess each Canon separately over a three-week cycle.

During the first week you teach and assess Invention by providing immediate feedback on their exercise pages and their ANI charts.

During the second week, you teach Arrangement. Before your students begin to write their essays (Elocution), you will provide feedback on their Arrangement exercise pages and outlines.

During the third week, you teach Elocution. You will provide prompt feedback on their exercise pages, and then review their essays after they have added the new materials. They will turn in their completed essays on the assigned date, and you will return them promptly with appropriate feedback.

Here's a table to clarify what it looks like:

	Invention (week one)	**Arrangement (week two)**	**Elocution (week three)**
Practice	Informally review student exercises and exercise pages	Informally review student exercises and exercise pages	Informally review student exercises and exercise pages
Performance	Review ANI charts and provide immediate	Review outline and worksheets and provide immediate	Review the essay draft and give immediate feedback

	feedback	feedback	
Product	Formally Review completed ANI charts	Formally Review completed outlines	Formally Assess the completed essays

When you review your students' product for each canon, you will note whether they have completed the work as required. If they have, return their papers to them with an A (for Accepted or Accomplished).

If not, return the paper with an I for "incomplete" and provide necessary feedback, including specific instructions that explain how to complete the assignment to demonstrate mastery of the specific skill learned. This should become a habit for your students.

When they return the paper with the needed corrections, mark it with an A and return it with congratulations.

Limiting grades to an "A" or an "I" simplifies grading and directs your students to things they can do. It also enables you to provide actionable feedback: the task was done up to the standard or it was not. If it was not, outline what needs to be done.

DETAILED STEPS FOR ASSESSING THE CANONS

To assess what your students have done in each canon, conduct the following steps:

- ❖ Assess their invention materials
  Assessment of Invention can be summarized by these three questions:

  - Were all instructions followed and requirements fulfilled?

  - Were the Exercises completed correctly?

  - Was gathered information moved to the ANI chart?

- ❖ Assess their Arrangement materials
  Assessment of Arrangement can be summarized by these three questions:

- Were the Exercises executed correctly?
- Was each part of the worksheet completed correctly?
- Did your students' outline follow the template exactly?

❖ Assess the Elocution materials and the essay itself
  Assessment of Elocution can be summarized by these three steps:

- Were the Elocution exercises executed correctly?

- Read the essay itself as follows:

    o First, orient yourself to the essay by reading it quickly. If you can avoid knowing who wrote the essay, do so.

    o Next, survey the essay to identify the structure. Ensure that it follows the outline. You may find it helpful to put a symbol next to each part of the essay and compare it with the template. For example, you might write "amp" in the margin to note that your student has included the amplification where it belongs.

    o Next, scan the essay for correct spelling, grammar, and punctuation. When it comes to grammar and usage, you should mark every mistake, whether you have taught the correct forms or not. Do not take points off for an error unless you know it has been taught, but do require students to fix mistakes so they don't become bad habits. If necessary use this opportunity to teach them correct grammar and usage. Give them the time needed to learn new things.

    o Next, scan the essay to find the required Elocution elements (e.g. parallelism, similes, etc.)

    o Finally, read the whole essay. Is it clear and coherent? What has your student done that is noteworthy?

Read with a red pen in your hand, noting things right and wrong. If something is wrong, show your students their errors and how to correct them. If things are well

done, honor them. Offer your students the objective, actionable criticism and affirmation they need to grow. Growing can hurt, but it also makes us happy.

GRADING WITH NUMBERS OR LETTERS

In some situations you may be required to give letter or number grades to your students. In that case, we recommend that you use the forms and procedures laid out below.

If you must give a letter or number grade, do not base it on how well they practiced their exercises. Practice is for making mistakes and getting better. Good practice will lead to good performance and thus to good grades.

What to Look for

For the final grade, divide your students' work into five categories, each of which is worth a total of 20 points. These categories are, for the most part, very objective. They are:

- Invention
- Arrangement
- Elocution
- Mechanics
- Thought

Invention

Under Invention you are looking for evidence that your students understood and performed the required tasks. If you teach them the ANI columns and require them to write fifteen facts in each column, then you grade them accordingly. The 15 facts in each column are worth a total of twenty points. If you require them to define their words following the steps of the Definition Worksheet and they do so, give them twenty points.

The number of required tasks will grow as you proceed, so your students may eventually score only five points for definition, while scoring, for example, five more for comparison, five for the ANI columns, and five for circumstances. Adjust the scores to match the required tasks.

While teaching LTW I, you should emphasize quantity and procedures when you assess Invention.

Arrangement

Under Arrangement, assess how thoroughly and accurately your students complied with the worksheet and template instructions. If they completed the worksheet without omission or error, and if they converted the worksheet into an outline by exactly following the template, they should receive 20 points for Arrangement.

Elocution

Elocution can be divided into three divisions: Elocution proper, or expression; mechanics; and thought. Elocution includes what is usually graded in an essay. The teacher asks: "How well did my students express their thoughts?" You should concentrate on whether students have included the tools you have taught them. While elocution requires more judgment and discretion than Invention and Arrangement, it still rests on an objective foundation. If you taught your students the scheme of alliteration, did they use it correctly? What else did you require? Did they fulfill your requirements? If so, they should receive full credit for doing so.

Mechanics

Under Mechanics, you are looking for four things: Did your students follow instructions (including layout, heading, etc.), is the work unified (is it about one thing or does it wander from subject to subject?), and, are the grammar and spelling correct? Each of these four elements is worth five points.

Thought

Under Thought you are looking for four things as well: are the writers' thoughts expressed clearly? Are the ideas adequately supported? Is the content appropriate and sufficient? Does the paper show insight on the part of the writer? Each of these four elements is worth five points.

ASSESSMENT RUBRIC

Here is a rubric you can copy if you must give number grades. We recommend that you not tell students their score until they have read the details of the assessment and that you make very clear to them how they can improve their work. Feel free to photocopy this page as many times as necessary.

Mechanics

    Followed Instructions

    Unity

    Grammar

    Spelling

Thought

    Clarity

    Support

    Insight

    Content

Invention

Arrangement

Elocution

APPENDIX C
ESSAY TEMPLATES

ESSAY ONE: RUDIMENTARY PERSUASIVE OUTLINE

I. Introduction
    A. Thesis*

    B. Enumeration*

    C. Exposition
        1. Proof I*
        2. Proof II*
        3. Proof III*

II. Proof
    A. Proof 1*

    B. Proof 2*

    C. Proof 3*

III. Conclusion
    A. Thesis*

    B. Summary of Proof
        1. Proof I*
        2. Proof II*
        3. Proof III*

ESSAY TWO: INTRODUCTORY PERSUASIVE OUTLINE

I. Introduction
  A. Thesis*

  B. Enumeration*

  C. Exposition
    1. Proof I*
    2. Proof II*
    3. Proof III*

II. Proof
  A. Proof I*
    1. Sub-proof 1*
    2. Sub-proof 2*
    3. Sub-proof 3*
  B. Proof II*
    1. Sub-proof 1*
    2. Sub-proof 2*
    3. Sub-proof 3*
  C. Proof III*
    1. Sub-proof 1*
    2. Sub-proof 2*
    3. Sub-proof 3*

III. Conclusion
  A. Thesis*

  B. Summary of Proof
    1. Proof I*
    2. Proof II*
    3. Proof III*

ESSAY THREE: INTRODUCTORY PERSUASIVE OUTLINE

I. Introduction

    A. Exordium *
    B. Thesis*
    C. Enumeration*
    D. Exposition
        1. Proof I*
        2. Proof II*
        3. Proof III*

II. Proof

    A. Proof I*
        1. Sub-proof 1*
        2. Sub-proof 2*
        3. Sub-proof 3*
    B. Proof II*
        1. Sub-proof 1*
        2. Sub-proof 2*
        3. Sub-proof 3*
    C. Proof III*
        1. Sub-proof 1*
        2. Sub-proof 2*
        3. Sub-proof 3*

III. Conclusion

    A. Thesis*

    B. Summary of Proof
        1. Proof I*
        2. Proof II*
        3. Proof III*

ESSAY FOUR: INTRODUCTORY PERSUASIVE OUTLINE

I. Introduction
    A. Exordium *
    B. Thesis *
    C. Enumeration *
    D. Exposition
        1. Proof I*
        2. Proof II*
        3. Proof III*

II. Proof
    A. Proof I*
        1. Sub-proof 1*
        2. Sub-proof 2*
        3. Sub-proof 3*
    B. Proof II*
        1. Sub-proof 1*
        2. Sub-proof 2*
        3. Sub-proof 3*
    C. Proof III*
        1. Sub-proof 1*
        2. Sub-proof 2*
        3. Sub-proof 3*

III. Conclusion
    A. Thesis*
    B. Summary of Proof
        1. Proof I*
        2. Proof II*
        3. Proof III*

ESSAY FIVE: INTRODUCTORY PERSUASIVE OUTLINE

I. Introduction
    A. Exordium *
    B. Division
        1. Agreement *
        2. Disagreement
            a. Thesis *
            b. Counter-thesis *
    C. Distribution
        1. Thesis *
        2. Enumeration *
        3. Exposition
            a. Proof I*
            b. Proof II*
            c. Proof III*

II. Proof
    A. Proof I*
        1. Sub-proof 1*
        2. Sub-proof 2*
        3. Sub-proof 3*
    B. Proof II*
        1. Sub-proof 1*
        2. Sub-proof 2*
        3. Sub-proof 3*
    C. Proof III*
        1. Sub-proof 1*
        2. Sub-proof 2*
        3. Sub-proof 3*

III. Conclusion
    A. Thesis*
    B. Summary of Proof
        1. Proof I*
        2. Proof II*
        3. Proof III*
    C. Amplification
        1. To Whom It Matters*
        2. Why It Matters To That Person or Group*

ESSAY SIX: INTRODUCTORY PERSUASIVE OUTLINE

I. Introduction

    A. Exordium *
    B. Division
        1. Agreement *
        2. Disagreement
            a. Thesis *
            b. Counter-thesis *
    C. Distribution
        1. Thesis *
        2. Enumeration *
        3. Exposition
            a. Proof I*
            b. Proof II*
            c. Proof III*

II. Proof
    A. Proof I*
        1. Sub-proof 1*
        2. Sub-proof 2*
        3. Sub-proof 3*
    B. Proof II*
        1. Sub-proof 1*
        2. Sub-proof 2*
        3. Sub-proof 3*
    C. Proof III*
        1. Sub-proof 1*
        2. Sub-proof 2*
        3. Sub-proof 3*

III. Refutation
    A. Counter-Thesis *
    B. Counter-proof 1 *
        1. Summary of support for reason 1 (in one sentence) *
        2. Inadequacy of reason 1 *
    C. Counter-proof 2 *
        1. Summary of support for reason 2 (in one sentence)*
        2. Inadequacy of reason 2 *
    D. Summary of Refutation *

IV. Conclusion
    A. Thesis*
    B. Summary of Proof
        1. Proof I*
        2. Proof II*
        3. Proof III*
    C. Amplification
        1. To Whom It Matters*
        2. Why it matters*

ESSAYS SEVEN–NINE: COMPLETE PERSUASIVE OUTLINE

I. Introduction
- A. Exordium *
- B. Narratio
    1. Situation*
    2. Actions*
- C. Division
    1. Agreement *
    2. Disagreement
        a. Thesis *
        b. Counter-thesis *
- D. Distribution
    1. Thesis *
    2. Enumeration *
    3. Exposition
        a. Proof I*
        b. Proof II*
        c. Proof III*

II. Proof
- A. Proof I*
    1. Support 1*
    2. Support 2*
    3. Support 3*
- B. Proof II*
    1. Support 1*
    2. Support 2*
    3. Support 3*
- C. Proof III*
    1. Support 1*
    2. Support 2*
    3. Support 3*

III. Refutation
- A. Counter-Thesis *
- B. Counter-proof 1 *
    1. Summary of support for reason 1 (in one sentence) *
    2. Inadequacy of reason 1 *
- C. Counter-proof 2 *
    1. Summary of support for reason 2 (in one sentence)*
    2. Inadequacy of reason 2 *
- **D. Summary of Refutation ***

IV. Conclusion
- A. Thesis*
- B. Summary of Proof
    1. Proof I*
    2. Proof II*
    3. Proof III*
- C. Amplification
    1. To Whom It Matters *
    2. Why It Matters To That Person Or Group *

APPENDIX D
ON MIMETIC TEACHING

THE FIVE STAGES OF MIMETIC TEACHING

We recommend that you teach *The Lost Tools of Writing* following the mimetic mode of teaching, a five-stage sequence that corresponds to the way children naturally learn. Mimetic teaching is neither a series of immovable steps nor a collection of laws; instead it follows the very flexible and adaptable natural stages students move through when they come to understand and master ideas and skills.

To teach mimetically, the teacher must first embrace the goal of the lesson: that the student will be able to apply the idea being taught. Therefore, each Lesson Guide clearly expresses to the teacher the ideas and skills contained in the lesson and equips you to teach them effectively.

As these Lesson Guides deepen your understanding, you will find yourself able to generate additional ideas of your own as examples, questions, practice, and so on. The Lesson Guides are not your master; they are your tool.

The Lesson Guides present each lesson in the following sequence (The Stages of the Lesson):

- **Preparation**
- **Presentation** of types (examples or illustrations)
- **Comparison** of types
- **Expression** of the idea by the students
- **Application** of the idea by the students

Remember, you will be able to teach the lessons effectively if you understand each lesson's core idea. You will find that in the Lesson Guides. Let it guide your class instruction and your students' practice.

PREPARATION: PREPARING THE STUDENTS FOR THE NEW IDEA

Can you think of a time when you wanted to teach a lesson, but you weren't sure your students were ready for it? What did you do? If it worked, you intuitively led them through the preparation stage.

Your goal in the preparation stage is to prepare your students to receive the new idea by making them aware of what they already know about the lesson and by generating a need within them for the idea it contains. For example, when teaching metaphors, you might review the lesson on how to generate similes since, if they can generate similes, they are ready to learn how to generate metaphors.

Or when you teach them how to generate parallel phrases, you might ask them to identify the parts of speech, to generate a series of parallel words, and to explain what a phrase is.. Now you know that they know almost everything contained in the lesson. At this point, you can create a need within them for parallel phrases by showing them incoherent or awkward phrases, possibly even some they have written. Now they are ready and willing to continue to the next stage.

Take your time on this preparation stage. It will seem to slow things down. In fact, the more they know what they already know, and the more you know what they don't, the better and more permanently you can link the new to old knowledge, and the more quickly you will be able to move through the later stages of Mimetic teaching.

> Prepare your students for the new idea by asking them what they already know

Many benefits arise from this first stage, including more engaged students possessing the confidence that they can learn and apply the new tools (after all, they already know almost everything they need to know!) and, for you the teacher, the opportunity to promptly and informally assess your students' readiness and to adapt appropriately.

PRESENTATION: PRESENTING THE TYPES

Your highest priority when you prepare this stage is to select or create types (specific examples or illustrations) that embody the idea you are teaching.

The Student Workbook contains many such types. For example, Elocution Worksheet 2, on parallelism, provides specific sentences and clauses written in a parallel structure.

COMPARISON: COMPARING THE TYPES

Once your students have seen several types, they are ready to compare them. In fact, they have already begun to do so, at least unconsciously, so your role is to guide them with questions like, "How is type A similar to type B?" and, "How is type A different from type B?" For example, when you compare examples of parallelism, you might ask "How is the first example similar to the second?" Later, you might ask, "What do all the parallel words, phrases, and clauses have in common?" Then, to sharpen and clarify the idea, you compare examples with counter-examples (i.e. parallel phrases with non-parallel phrase, metaphors with simple comparisons, alliteration with rhymes, etc.). Thus, by comparing types, your students come to see with their own eyes the idea the types embody.

As the teacher, you can use comparison questions to assess whether your students understand the types. If they are unable to compare, back up and re-present the types. Do not hurry!

EXPRESSION: EXPRESSION OF THE IDEA BY THE STUDENT

This stage is very short. You simply ask your students to describe or explain the idea. You might say, "Describe parallelism," or, "Explain how we define an object" or, "Explain how you will add Antithesis to your essay." The lesson guides have sample questions.

Ask multiple students to express the idea *in their own* words to ensure that your whole class has learned it. It often helps to ask students to write the idea so that all of them can express their thoughts without hearing their peers

If your students are unable to explain or describe the idea being taught, revert back to the third stage and compare the types more closely.

APPLICATION: STUDENTS PRACTICE THE IDEA LEARNED

During the application stage, your students apply what they have learned by completing a worksheet, template, or exercise, or essay. The Lesson Guides show you what to require of your students. Invention lessons show how to gather information, Arrangement lessons show how to order the information gathered, and Elocution lessons show how to refine their expression when they write the essay.

Note: Mimetic teaching is neither didactic (lecture-based) nor Socratic (question-based), though it uses both questions and direct instruction. Mimetic instruction guides students through the natural process of imitating an idea (that is, embodying a general concept in a specific instance). Since this summarizes what happens when a person learns something new, mimetic teaching develops habits that students internalize and can apply to every learning experience. Both the content and the form of The Lost Tools of Writing teach students how to think, write, and create. On top of all that, this mode of teaching is surprisingly efficient.

APPENDIX E
FAQS

1. What are the prerequisites for beginning this curriculum?

To optimize their use of *The Lost Tools of Writing*, students need to know the basics of grammar, including parts of speech, punctuation, and sentence construction. A student who can write a paragraph independently from scratch can learn and use the tools in this curriculum.

Students studying a foreign language, with a rich reading background, and who participate in discussions about books will find LTW aligns with and enriches their experiences.

2. Who Should Use *The Lost Tools of Writing*?

We recommend implementing *The Lost Tools of Writing* as follows:

- Any student in 9th grade or higher who has not learned these tools needs to learn them now. Without them, students simply have to work too hard.

- Any student in 7th or 8th grade who has a good background in grammar and basic writing is ready for LTW

- A student as young as 6th grade who has been writing quite a bit already and knows grammar well should begin LTW but should take at two years to complete it.

Every teacher needs to learn LTW Classical rhetoric is the integrating element of the curriculum so every teacher needs to know its tools and how to apply them to his or her subject matter.

3. How do I use this curriculum with younger students?

"Wisely and slow. They stumble that run fast." (Shakespeare, *Romeo & Juliet*) Consider taking a full two years to complete Level 1. Emphasize structure and the discipline of following the process.

Though the curriculum is geared to the student with a little writing background, middle school students who have experienced basic writing exercises and who know the elements of grammar are prepared for this program.

Teachers should begin using the tools of Invention as soon as they read to their students (pre-kindergarten). For example, the kindergarten teacher can and should ask whether the other animals should have followed Chicken Little, whether the ants should have given food to the grasshopper, and whether the Grinch should have taken little Cindy-Lou Who's Christmas tree. *The Lost Tools of Writing*™ is a classical rhetoric curriculum and effective teaching implements classical rhetoric.

We recommend you spend most of your time with young students building a strong foundation for future logic and rhetoric. Enjoy time reading great stories and books, delighting in poetry, learning the basics of grammar, and enjoying words together. This is the time to practice narration, sentence writing, and basic paragraph writing.

4. Is this curriculum only for classical schools?

If you desire to instill virtues of truth, goodness, and beauty while teaching children according to their natures, using a curriculum designed to promote skills in thinking and decision making, then *The Lost Tools of Writing*™ is for you. If all you want to do is teach them to write well, you won't find a better program – but we believe you are short-selling your students.

5. I'm not a writing teacher; I'm a homeschool mom. Am I qualified to teach this?

Homeschool moms are among our most satisfied customers because *The Lost Tools of Writing*™ builds better writers **and** teachers. We've put this program together in such a way that all you have to do is follow the process with your child.

6. Why don't you use familiar words like "hook"?

The Lost Tools of Writing™ is a course in classical rhetoric. We strive to gently introduce students to the language of the classical tradition so that when they read great books by authors like Aristotle, Shakespeare, etc. there is no language barrier.

Furthermore, we have found that the language of the classical curriculum is more effective because it is more objective and less prone to using subjectivist terms that work in one place but not in another. The strength of the language used leads to more precise thinking about writing, language, and the world that is named and discussed through language.

7. What about other kinds of writing besides the essay?

The Lost Tools of Writing™ lays foundations for every kind of writing and even speech in the persuasive essay. Writers who internalize the tools in Level One spend the rest of their lives applying and adapting them to different contexts, essay forms, poems, stories, or any specific instructor's requirements. The foundations remain. Refining a strong base of knowledge and skill is more effective than being exposed to more or less disconnected ideas without the time to master them.

Students learn stylistic techniques that they apply to reading and writing poetry; they cultivate a narrative sense to help them write stories; they practice gathering and evaluating testimony, the root of every form of research. Every essay practices logic, debate, and public speaking.

Truly, this curriculum offers the trunk of the Tree of Learning. Your students will never read, write, speak on, discuss, or make a decision about anything unaffected by *The Lost Tools of Writing*™.

8. Do I have to use this in conjunction with teaching literature?

No. While literature offers an abundance of issues about which to write essays (since every story turns on the decisions and actions of the characters), students with a rich reading diet have plenty of material to draw from. They can and should write essays about historical figures who made decisions as well. Should George Washington have crossed the Delaware? Should Brutus have assassinated Caesar?

This curriculum provides an integrating tool for the teacher who wishes to incorporate all of the student's studies and experiences into his scholarly reflections, thus reintegrating not only the school's curriculum but also the student's life.

Opportunities for writing and persuasive discourse abound. They are as close as your dining room table and last night's dinner discussion. Using literature, even a simple fable, offers the advantage of moving the discussion to a less personal sphere, but you are welcome to choose essay issues from any area of study. The world is rich with possibilities!

9. Does this curriculum teach literary analysis?

The Lost Tools of Writing™ teaches students how to read literature closely by asking the universal question that drives every story. By doing so, it prepares for and gives life back to literary analysis, which too often is experienced as a detached academic subject for specialists. Every student should be a reader; not all of them should be specialists. Those who become specialists must not lose sight of the universal nature of story.

Analysis is a special kind of writing that depends on the ability to read closely, think clearly, and express effectively. All three of these skills are taught in LTW, preparing any student to move on to more specialized kinds of writing. This curriculum is not an explicit literary analysis program. Instead it aims to equip students to grow in their appreciation, understanding, and communication of the great ideas in literature. At heart, every author seeks to persuade the reader, and those skills need to be mastered first. The tools of literary analysis are derived from the tools in this curriculum, however, so the student who completes *The Lost Tools of Writing*™ is more equipped for literary analysis than the student who attempts it without the foundational tools.

For example, the student who is taught about motifs and character arcs, but has never reflected on whether the character ought to do something, will never understand why the motif is there and why the arc rises at it does. That is why so many students are bored by literary analysis. They don't see the point.

10. How will this curriculum prepare my child for college?

See question 8 above. Additionally, anyone who knows how to arrange a paper can carry that skill into any situation. SAT writing, public speaking, research papers, and debate all benefit from a background in classical rhetoric.

College professors report to us that they are discouraged by the writing of most incoming freshmen. They also want more than five paragraph essays. The Lost Tools of Writing equips students to deal with any issue head on and to write an eleven paragraph essay that is easy to follow and easily expandable. The research paper, master's thesis, even the PhD thesis amount to extensions of the tools mastered through The Lost Tools of Writing.

Remember that The Lost Tools of Writing is classical rhetoric and classical rhetoric is the trunk of the tree of learning. There is no subject area that you cannot study more effectively by mastering these tools.

11. How do I grade the work?

Appropriate forms of assessment must be applied to master any skill, but to often the way we grade writing doesn't fit the nature of the art. Because we take assessment and feedback so seriously, we have included a guide to assessment in *The Lost Tools of Writing*™.

The only practical question when you are coaching a student is the twofold, "What milestone has my student reached and what comes next?" (How students compare to other students does not matter).

Each Essay Cycle contains a set of milestones and the guide to assessment explains how to assess whether each has been reached. Specific checklists are included with each lesson.

12. What if I can only meet with my students one day per week?

The Lost Tools of Writing™ has been used successfully in many different classroom and home situations. We recommend two or more meetings per week, but teachers have taught effectively in one class session per week as well. We present a once/week option in the Lesson Guides. Once you and the students are comfortable with the lesson sequence, you'll find the rhythm that works for you.

Think of it this way: You are teaching your students that each step of the writing process is worthy of a week's worth of thought and effort. If possible, encourage your students to communicate with you via email in order to accomplish incremental steps

13. Help! I'm confused.

Assistance is only a mouse-click away. First, we urge every LTW user to join our "LTW Mentor" email loop for access to fellow teachers, friendly advice, and files of student work. Mentor teachers, CiRCE Apprentices, headmasters, classroom teachers, and homeschool parents all contribute to the lively conversation. Years of good ideas have been collected and virtually every question that can be asked has been discussed in the Mentor, from the rudimentary to the most advanced. The LTW Mentor is really a LTW Community.

Next, visit The Lost Tools of Writing website for news and updates. You'll find information on LTW workshops, webinars, regional conferences, and other offerings to support LTW.

You'll never be alone when you use *The Lost Tools of Writing*.

APPENDIX F
GLOSSARY

Active voice: The verb form or voice in which the subject of the sentence performs or causes the action expressed by the verb.

Alliteration: A scheme involving the occurrence of the same letter or sound at the beginning of adjacent or closely connected words.

Amplification: Part of an essay's conclusion in which the writer states to whom his issue matters, and why it matters to that person or group.

Antecedent: An event that precedes another event, but does not necessarily cause it. We think about the antecedent when we apply the topic of Relation to the issue. "Ante" is from Latin, meaning "before." "Cede" is from Latin, meaning "to go."

Antithesis: A scheme in which strongly contrasting (or opposite) concepts are expressed in a parallel form.

Arrangement: The canon of composition by which the author orders the materials gathered in the Invention canon in a manner suited to the type of essay being written. It is sometimes called *dispositio*.

Arrangement Template: The pattern on which the outline is modeled; the structure of the essay in outline form.

Assonance: A rhetorical scheme in which a vowel sound is repeated in adjacent or closely connected words.

Common Topics: The Five Common Topics - Comparison, Definition, Circumstance, Relation, and Testimony – are places we go to gather information, from the Greek word, "topos," place.

Canon(s): The three fundamental activities of writing. They are Invention, Arrangement, and Elocution.

Cause: The actions, events, etc., that cause brought about the situation.

Circumstance: one of the Five Common Topics; Circumstance describes the actions and events that occur at the same time as, but in different locations from, the situation in which the issue arises.

Comparison: One of the Five Common Topics of Invention, Comparison asks how two terms (things, characters, places, ideas, etc.) are similar by noting what both terms "have", "are", and "do".

Conclusion: In writing, it is the ending of a text. It is prepared after the body of the text, and before the Introduction.

Consequent: An action that follows an event. This is part of the topic of Relation.

Counter-thesis: The statement of the position in direct opposition to the thesis

Definition: One of the five common topics. A definition of a word sets the limits within which a word has meaning. A definition of a thing identifies the genus and differentia of the thing defined. Definition asks the questions, "To what category does a thing belong?" "How does it compare to other members of that set?" and "What are its parts or aspects?" A formal definition states the genus (group) and differentia (unique qualities) of a term.

Differences of Degree: Differences of degree are expressed when one term is, has, or does more or less than other term. This is commonly expressed with the words more/less and better/worse.

Differences of Kind: Differences in kind are expressed when one term belongs to a group different than another term.

Differentiae: The differences between a term and the other members of its genus. In the topic of Definition, we ask what group (genus) our term belongs to, and how it is different from other members of the group.

Discovery: The first canon of rhetoric, during which the writer seeks and finds material for writing. This canon is also called Invention.

Disposition: The second canon of rhetoric, during which the writer sorts and arranges materials gather during Invention. This canon is also called Arrangement, or *dispositio*.

Distribution: The portion of the Division that states the thesis, enumeration, and exposition.

Division: A precise statement of the agreement and disagreement between the writer and an opponent.

Effect: The result of an action or cause.

Elocution: The third canon of rhetoric in which the writer selects the appropriate words and forms to best express the ideas of the text. This canon is also called Style.

Enumeration: A statement of the number of reasons you will use to support your thesis statement.

Essay Cycle: A complete set of teaching material for one essay that includes all three canons. This curriculum contains 10 lessons, with the first as an introduction. The 9 lessons in the middle will each take three weeks to teach.

Exercise: An action or series of actions by which the student practices the skill he is learning.

Exordium: The opening of an essay or speech, placed at the beginning of the introduction. Its purpose is to make the audience receptive to the speech or essay so they will listen.

Exposition: A statement of the main points in an essay or speech.

Genus: The category or group to which the thing defined belongs; the first part of a term's definition.

Idea: The universal concept that is abstracted out of individual types by a process of comparison. The meaning of an idea can never be exhausted.

Interesting Column: The column on the ANI chart used to record ideas generated during the Invention process that are not clearly Affirmative or Negative.

All the information students generate during Invention that does not belong to the "A" or "N" column should be considered part of the "I" column, even if they do not copy it onto the chart.

Introduction: The first part of an essay, developed after the body and the Conclusion of the essay are written.

Invention: The first canon of rhetoric during which the writer discovers material (an inventory) for the text. This canon is also called Discovery; coming up with something to say when we write.

Issue: A question converted to a whether statement. The Issue serves to generate questions about both the affirmative and negative responses to the question. Students generate a new issue for each new essay.

Lesson Guide: An independent lesson that teaches one tool or idea from the canon of which it is a part.

Metaphor: a trope, is an indirect comparison of two different kinds of things. (indirect- i.e. you do not use like or as).

Narratio: Narrative; also called a "statement of facts" or "statement of circumstances". It tells a story, with settings, actors, and actions, to inform the reader about the circumstances they need to know about the subject, or thesis, of the essay.

Parallelism: A similarity of structure in a pair or series of related words, phrases, or clauses (sentences).

Passive voice: a verb form or voice in which the grammatical subject receives the verb's action.

Part of speech: One of the traditional categories of words intended to reflect their grammatical functions of the words: nouns, pronouns, adjectives, verbs, adverbs, prepositions, interjections, and conjunctions.

Proof: This term has two uses in *The Lost Tools of Writing*™: 1) The body of an essay; it contains the main arguments or reasons, with their supports, for the thesis. 2) The main reasons that make up the "proof" of the first sense. Each main reason includes three "sub-proofs."

Proposition: The judgment expressed by a statement. Its predicate affirms or denies something about its subject. It is either true or false.

Question: An interrogative sentence in which a speaker seeks information or confirmation. A question is the starting point of thought, and therefore, of each essay.

Reason: An argument or proof in defense of a thesis.

Refutation: The response to an opposing argument. For the persuasive essay, you anticipate two arguments that your opponent will have against your thesis. A refutation states those two counter-proofs and why they are inadequate.

Relation: one of the Five Common Topics; Relation lists events or actions that take place before and after the situation in which the issue arises and determines which are causes of the situation and which could be the effects of the actor's decisions (for or against).

Scheme: An arrangement of words or letters appealing to the senses (along with tropes, sometimes called "figures of speech"), e.g., a rhyme scheme.

Simile: Simile is a trope that makes an explicit comparison of two things different in kind but sharing a common characteristic. It uses words as "like" or "as" to make the comparison.

Situation: The setting, actors, and dilemma in which the Issue arises. The situation is developed much further in the lessons on Narratio and Relation.

Species: Other members of the group ("genus") that a term (in an issue) belongs to. In logic, these are specific things that are members of the genus, or group.

Style: Also called Elocution.

Summary: A brief statement of the totality of all the ideas presented. In a Persuasive Essay, the summary is in the conclusion. It includes the thesis and three main reasons.

Teacher: One who mediates an idea from his soul to the soul of a student.

Teaching: Mediating an idea from one soul to another.

Template: A pattern. The template is the form to imitate when we make an outline for our essays.

Terms: Word or expression used to name a thing.

Testimony: One of the five common topics; sometimes this topic is called Authority. Testimony asks witnesses what they know about the situation or event.

Thesis: The statement of the proposition defended by an essay. A thesis is derived from a question when the writer: 1) converts the question to an issue, 2) decides which side to defend, and 3) restates the issue as a statement representing the affirmative or negative position.

Topics: Question we ask in order to come up with something to say when we write.

Trope: An arrangement of words appealing to the mind or imagination (along with schemes, sometimes called "figures of speech"), e.g., a metaphor.

Type: An example or model from which something is made.

Universal: An idea or concept that is drawn out of (abstracted from) the particulars or types. For example, we learn "blue, red, yellow" as particulars, and then we understand the universal idea of "color." The universal is what all the particulars have in common.

Worksheet: In this curriculum, a worksheet is the form that guides the student or teacher through a pattern that they will learn to imitate. The goal of a worksheet is to help a person internalize a pattern of thinking so that the worksheet is no longer needed.

APPENDIX G
RESOURCES

1. ESSENTIAL RESOURCES

Corbett, Edward P.J. *Classical Rhetoric for the Modern Student.* New York: Oxford University Press, 1990.

Crider, Scott F. *The Office Of Assertion: An Art of Rhetoric for the Academic Essay,* Wilmington, Del: ISI Books, 2005

Strunk, William, Jr. and E.B. White. *Elements of Style.* Fourth Edition. Boston: Longman, 2000.

2. RECOMMENDED RESOURCES

Adler, Mortimer J. *Aristotle for Everybody.* New York: Bantam Books, 1980.

Berry, Wendell. *Standing by Words.* Washington, DC: Shoemaker & Hoard, 2005.

Bizzell, Patricia and Bruce Herzberg, eds. *The Rhetorical Tradition: Readings from Classical Times to the Present.* Boston: Bedford, St. Martin's, 2001.

Cicero. *AD C. Herennium Libri IV, De Ratione Dicendi.* Translated by Harry Caplan. Loeb Classical Library. No. 403. Cambridge, MA: Harvard University Press, 1981.

Colman, John E. *The Master Teachers and the Art of Teaching.* New York: Pitman Publishing Corporation, 1967.

Cothran, Martin. *Classical Rhetoric with Aristotle.* Classical Trivium Core Series. Memoria Press, 2002–05.

Crowley, Sharon and Debra Hawhee. *Ancient Rhetorics for Contemporary Students.* Needham Heights, Massachusetts: Allyn & Bacon, 1999.

de Bono, Edward. *de Bono's Thinking Course.* New York: Facts on File Publications, 1985.

Flesch, Rudolf. *The Art of Plain Talk.* New York: Harper & Brothers Publishers, 1946.

Gregory, John Milton. *The Seven Laws of Teaching.* Grand Rapids, Michigan: Baker Book House, 1993.

Hicks, David V. *Norms and Nobility: A Treatise on Education.* Savage, Maryland: Rowman & Littlefield Publishers, Inc., 1991.

Horner, Winifred Bryan. *Rhetoric in the Classical Tradition.* New York: St. Martin's Press, 1988.

Joseph, Sister Miriam. *Shakespeare's Use of the Arts of Language.* Philadelphia: Paul Dry Books, 2005.

Joseph, Sister Miriam. *The Trivium: The Liberal Arts of Logic, Grammar, and Rhetoric.* Philadelphia: Paul Dry Books, 2002.

Kirszner, Laurie G. and Stephen R. Mandell. *The Holt Handbook.* Third Edition. Fort Worth, TX: Harcourt Brace College Publishers, 1986.

McMurry, Charles A. and Frank M. McMurry. *The Method of the Recitation.* New York: The MacMillan Company, 1905.

Mason, Charlotte. *A Philosophy of Education.* Vol. 6. Wheaton, Illinois: Tyndale House Publishers, Inc., 1989.

Meyer, Herbert and Jill. *How to Write: Communicating Ideas and Information.* New York: Barnes & Noble Books, 1993.

Murphy, J. P. *Conversation.* Philadelphia: The Penn Publishing Company, 1911.

Percival, Milton and R. A. Jelliffe. *Specimens of Exposition and Argument.* New York: The MacMillan Company, 1908.

Quiller-Couch, Sir Arthur. *On the Art of Writing.* New York: G. P. Putnam's Sons, 1943.

Quinn, Arthur. *Figures of Speech: 60 Ways to Turn a Phrase.* Salt Lake City: Gibbs M. Smith, Inc., 1982.

"Silva Rhetoricae: The Forest of Rhetoric." Brigham Young University. http://humanities.byu.edu/rhetoric/silva.htm

Spangler, Mary Michael, O.P. *Aristotle on Teaching.* New York: University Press of America, Inc., 1998.

Veith, Gene Edward, Jr. and Andrew Kern. *Classical Education: The Movement Sweeping America.* Washington, DC: Capital Research Center, 2001.

Whately, Richard. *Elements of Rhetoric.* Douglas Ehninger, ed. Carbondale, Illinois: Southern Illinois University Press, 1963.

Williams, Joseph M. *Style: Ten Lessons in Clarity and Grace*. Fifth Edition. New York: Addison-Wesley Educational Publishers, Inc., 1997.

3. ADVANCED RESOURCES

Adams, John Quincy. *Lectures on Rhetoric and Oratory*. Scholars' Facsimiles and Reprints, June 1997.

Alpers, Paul J. *Elizabethan Poetry: Modern Essays in Criticism*. New York: Oxford University Press, 1967.

Aristotle. *"Art" of Rhetoric*. Loeb Classical Library. Translated by John Henry Freese. No. 193. Cambridge, MA: Harvard University Press, 1982.

_____. *Categories, On Interpretation, Prior Analytics*. Translated by H. P. Cooke and H. Tredennick. Loeb Classical Library. No. 325. Cambridge, MA: Harvard University Press, 1973.

_____. *"Longinus" on the Sublime, Demetrius on Style*. Translated by W. Hamilton Fyfe and W. Rhys Roberts. Loeb Classical Library. No. 199. Cambridge, MA: Harvard University Press, 1973.

_____. *Posterior Analytics, Topica*. Translated by H. Tredennick and E. S. Forster. Loeb Classical Library. No. 391. Cambridge, MA: Harvard University Press, 1960.

Cicero. *De Inventione, De Optimo Genere Oratorum, Topica*. Translated by H. M. Hubbell. Loeb Classical Library. No. 386. Cambridge, MA: Harvard University Press, 1976.

_____. *De Oratore: Books I and II*. Translated by H. Rackham and E. W. Sutton. Loeb Classical Library. No. 349. Cambridge, MA: Harvard University Press, 2001.

_____. *De Oratore: De Fato, Paradoxa Stoicorum, De Partitione Oratoria*. Translated by H. Rackham. Loeb Classical Library. No. 348. Cambridge, MA: Harvard University Press, 1988.

Quintilian. *The Institutio Oratoria*. Book 1. Translated by H. E. Butler. Loeb Classical Library. No. 124. Cambridge, MA: Harvard University Press, 1980.

_____. Book 2. Translated by Donald A. Russell. Loeb Classical Library. No. 125. Cambridge, MA: Harvard University Press, 2001.

_____. Book 3. Translated by Donald A. Russell. Loeb Classical Library. No. 126. Cambridge, MA: Harvard University Press, 2001.

———. Book 4. Translated by Donald A. Russell. Loeb Classical Library. No. 127. Cambridge, MA: Harvard University Press, 2001.

———. Book 5. Translated by Donald A. Russell. Loeb Classical Library. No. 494. Cambridge, MA: Harvard University Press, 2001.

APPENDIX H
LESSON SUMMARIES

ESSAY ONE

Invention: From Question to ANI
Essay One Invention teaches the first two steps for writing a persuasive essay:

1. *Turn a question into an Issue.*
2. *Discover basic information by filling out the ANI chart.*

To turn a question into an Issue, restate the question as a phrase that begins with the word "whether." For example, if your question is, "Should Edmund have followed the White Witch?" your Issue is, "Whether Edmund should have followed the White Witch." If your question is, "Was Achilles right to be angry with Agamemnon?" your Issue is, "Whether Achilles was right to be angry with Agamemnon."

The next step is to discover and organize information related to the Issue according to whether it argues for or against the issue, or whether it is argues for neither. To do this, complete the ANI chart (ANI stands for Affirmative, Negative, and Interesting). If a piece of information argues for the Affirmative, place it in the A column. If it argues for the Negative, place it in the N column. If it is simply an interesting fact, place it in the I column.

For example, if your issue is, "Whether Edmund should have followed the White Witch," in the A column, you might place bits of information like this: she gave him Turkish Delight, he didn't know she was a witch, he was cold and hungry, he was lost. In the N column, you might place information like this: Lucy had warned him about her, she wasn't kind to her horses or the dwarf, she yelled at Edmund, he would be sneaking away from his siblings. In the I column, place interesting pieces of information: the White Witch had a sled, it was winter, he and his siblings had been playing hide-and-go-seek, and she was very tall.

These first two steps - creating an issue out of a question and completing the ANI chart - lay the foundation for the persuasive essay.

Arrangement: From ANI to Outline
Essay One Arrangement introduces a number of names for the parts of an essay, including *Proof, Thesis, Introduction, Conclusion, Enumeration,* and *Exposition.* The *Thesis* is the statement that the essay defends. The *Proof* states the main reasons for the Thesis. If the Issue is, "Whether Edmund should have followed

the White Witch," the Negative Thesis is, "Edmund should not have followed the White Witch." The Proof then lists three reasons that support the Negative position.

The *Introduction* is the opening to an essay and the *Conclusion* summarizes the essay by reviewing the argument. The *Enumeration* is the number of reasons the essay presents in support of its thesis and the *Exposition* presents the main points that make up the Proof.

Arrangement One presents an Arrangement Template that organizes these elements into a Rudimentary Persuasive Essay.. It lays a foundation on which ensuing essays grow.

Elocution: From Outline to Text
While the Student Workbook does *not* contain a worksheet for Elocution One, but you will learn to turn the outline from Arrangement One into a Rudimentary Persuasive Essay. You do this by making complete sentences out of the phrases and key words used in their outlines.

The first Rudimentary Persuasive Essay prioritizes structure, not eloquence. It initiates the discipline that the rest of the essays will demand. Do not worry about this essay sounding good, but about it being organized according to the proper structure.

ESSAY TWO

Invention: Introduction to the Five Topics
Essay Two briefly introduces the Five Topics of Invention. The Five Topics are tools for gathering information. The Topics are **Comparison, Definition, Circumstance, Relation,** and **Testimony**. Central to classical rhetoric, each of these five topics contains sub-questions that help the essay writer generate information pertaining to the issue.

The topic of **Comparison** asks, "How is X similar to Y?" and, "How is X different from Y?" For example, the writer might compare Edmund to Peter by asking how Edmund is similar to Peter. They are both brothers to Lucy and Susan, they are both British males, and they both go to Narnia. Also, both are characters in the book. However, they are different in that Peter is older, is less mean to Lucy, and does not sneak away from the group.

The topic of **Definition** asks, "Who or what is X?" and, "What kind of thing is X?" If X is Edmund, we might say that he is a boy from England who is in *The Lion, the Witch, and the Wardrobe*. We might also say that he is a brother and a son, that he becomes a king, and that he is a character in a book.

Circumstance asks, "What was happening at the time of the situation?" If we ask about the issue discussed above, we might ask, "What was happening in Narnia when Edmund met the White Witch?" and we might answer by recalling that Narnia was in the middle of a 100-year winter or that the White Witch was turning creatures into stone. We might also ask, "What was happening in England, Europe, or Calormen at that time?"

Relation asks what happened before and after the situation in which the issue arose. It is particularly interested in cause and effect. If we ask, "What happened immediately before and after Edmund followed the White Witch?" we might respond by recalling that Edmund and his siblings had been sent to stay with an older professor during the war and that they had been arguing about whether Lucy was just imagining Narnia. Afterward, we might note, they became kings and queens of Narnia.

Finally, **Testimony** asks, "What do witnesses say about the issue?" We might ask what Tumnus, a witness to the actions and character of the White Witch, can offer as testimony.

These topics and their accompanying questions are powerful tools to help the student complete an ANI chart and discover ideas. More significantly, they are universal, powerful tools for anybody who has a decision to make.

Arrangement A: A Guide To Sorting
In Essay Two Arrangement you will learn to sort and categorize the information on the ANI charts into groups by using symbols, such as @, $, or &. To do this, place a symbol of their choosing next to the first item in the affirmative and negative columns. Determine which items in each column might be organized into the same group as the first item. Place the same symbol next to all of the items that fit into this group. Follow the same process for every item in each column until every item has a corresponding symbol next to it. Each symbol thus corresponds to a group into which the items in the columns have been catalogued.

Next, choose an appropriate heading, or name, for each group. Then select three groups that have at least three members each. Those groups become the Proofs and the group members become the Sub-Proofs. Reviewing those Proofs, choose the side of the Issue - the Affirmative or the Negative – that you will defend.

Arrangement B: Introductory Persuasive Essay Outline. In Essay Two, you add Sub-Proofs to each of the three Proofs. Using the items sorted with Arrangement Worksheet A, fill out Worksheet B and its corresponding template to create a slightly more complicated outline than the Essay One version.

Elocution: Scheme – Parallelism 1: Words
Parallelism, a scheme, is a similarity of structure in a pair or series of related words, phrases, or clauses.

For example, when writers form a list in a sentence, each item in the list should be the same part of speech. When they combine phrases with a semi-colon, the grammatical structure of the two phrases should be identical.

Parallelism gives harmonious form, interest, and beauty to a sentence or passage. For example, consider the following correct usage of parallelism:

"Ronald Reagan was an actor, a governor, and a president."

On the other hand, consider the following non-parallel sentence (error in bold):

Ronald Reagan was an actor, a governor, **and then he presided over the country.**

ESSAY THREE

Invention: Comparison - Similarities
Essay Three Invention introduces Comparison, one of the Common Topics. The topic of Comparison invites the student to discover similarities between two terms by examining what both terms **are, have, and do.**

For example, both Edmund and the White Witch are human-like beings, both have relationships, and both do harm to others.

Arrangement: A Guide to Exordium
Every essay should open with something to catch the reader's attention and set the tone for the rest of the essay. This opening is called the Exordium, and in Essay Three Arrangement you learn three types of Exordium: the **question**, the **challenge**, and the quotation. When used properly, each can pique the interest and attention of the reader before you have even presented your Thesis.

In an essay about whether Edmund should have followed the White Witch, you might ask a question like, "Have you ever been tempted by something that seemed too good to be true?" or "Have you ever been misled by someone who seemed good?"

You might challenge readers to never do anything wrong again or to do something as simple as "Listen!" or "Lend me your ears." Any imperative statement directed at the audience is a challenge to them.
To begin with a quotation, you could present a text from the Bible on the dangers of pride or from a famous writer on the dangers of following leaders who buy your loyalty.

Elocution: Basic Editing - Verbs
This lesson focuses on two common verb problems: passive verbs and vague verbs. You should avoid them and replace them with more active and precise verbs. Passive verbs should be avoided because they tend to obscure the actor, while vague verbs communicate less meaning than more precise verbs.

A passive verb is a verb in which the subject of the sentence is not acting but is being acted upon. For example, in the sentence, "The book was lost by the man," the subject - the book - is not acting, but is being acted upon. It would usually be better to say, "The man lost the book."

Vague verbs lack specificity, so they are common, like *are, do, have, got, went, etc.* as in, "He got himself closer to the window." Sometimes, vague verbs are aided by helping verbs, as in "Ickey does a dance." It would usually be better to say, "Ickey dances," or "He drew closer to the window," or even, "He approached the window." Do a hunt for unnecessary helping verbs and get overly common verbs and you'll find plenty of vague verbs to replace.

Strong verbs are the life-blood of a sentence. Without vigorous, energetic, specific verbs, a sentence struggles to express the writer's ideas.

ESSAY FOUR

Invention: Comparison - Degree and Kind
As you learned in Essay Three, you can compare any two items by looking for their similarities: asking what both terms are, have, and do. In Essay Four Invention, you compare terms to find differences.

Things can differ in two ways: one can be, have, or do more or less than the other, or one can be, have, or do a different kind of thing from the other. The first is a difference of degree, the second a difference of kind.

The most obvious way to find differences is simply to ask how the terms are different and to note the differences identified. That is a good place to start. But in this lesson, you learn to refine the search.

To find Comparisons of Degree and Kind, first, find similarities between two terms, as you did in Comparison One. Then draw differences of degree or kind from the similarities.

For instance, a pen and a pencil are both writing instruments. To find a difference of degree, ask which one is better and why or which one has more of something than the other (such as length) and by how much. Of course, the normal way to ask the second question is to ask which is longer, a difference of degree.

Both Edmund and the White Witch are living beings. To find a difference in kind, ask what kind of living being Edmund is (human boy) and then ask what kind of living being the White Witch is (purportedly a half jinn-half giant woman).

Arrangement: A Guide to Amplification
Amplification is a concluding statement that answers the questions, *Who cares?* and, *Why?* To write an Amplification, first identify the audience to whom the essay or speech is addressed. Then identify a group about whom that audience cares and how the decision might affect them.

The audience could be the writer's friends, Mr. Tumnus, or even the teacher. Groups the audience cares about could be family, the Narnians, or the teacher's students. The decision could affect these groups in various ways, among them:

the Narnians could be permanently subjected to the White Witch if Edmund follows her and betray his siblings. It is for the writer to determine which audience to address, which group that audience cares about, and how the decision might affect them.

ESSAY FIVE

Invention: Definition I

Essay Five focuses on the Topic of Definition. You define a thing or idea by identifying the group it belongs to and how it is different from all the other members of that group.

For each essay, you will define one or more terms from your issue. A *term* is a word or phrase that names a particular thing (a person, idea, place, emotion, etc.) or a particular action. If you are writing about the issue, "Whether Edmund should have followed the White Witch," your terms are the words *Edmund, followed, and White Witch*. Words like articles and helping verbs are technically terms as well, but you do not need to define them.

To define the term *Edmund:*

> -Identify what kind of thing *Edmund* is. What is he? He is a boy, a citizen of Great Britain, a brother and son, and a character in a book.

> -Decide which of these groups will be most helpful as you think about the term in the context of this essay. For the sake of simplicity, let's choose *boys* as the group to examine.

> -Identify other members of the group *boys*, such as Peter (Edmund's brother), Tom Sawyer, Dennis the Menace, Harry Potter, or Charlie Brown.

> -Consider why each member of the list above is a member of the group *boys*. Identify properties or characteristics they all share. So we might identify them as older than babies but younger than men.

> -Identify characteristics that make the term *Edmund* different from every other member of the group *boys*. These characteristics are called

differentia, and the writer needs them to differentiate this Edmund from any others. We might say that Edmund was a character in this particular book, that he was Peter's younger brother, that he was a king of Narnia, or that he was motivated by envy.

To write the definition for the term *Edmund,* we include only the term, its group, and its necessary differences. *Edmund is a boy, the younger brother of Peter Pevensie, motivated by envy.*

Arrangement: A Guide to Division
Division identifies the point of disagreement between the writer and those who hold the opposing view. The purpose of the Division is to clarify the agreement and to specify the exact point of disagreement. After all, it is useless – and all too common - to debate a point upon which both sides agree.

To create the Division, follow these steps:

- Write the Thesis.
- Write the Counter-Thesis (the opposing position).
- Compare the two statements and determine areas where the sides agree.

For example, in an essay about whether Edmund should have followed the White Witch, the Thesis for the Negative would be, "Edmund should not have followed the White Witch," while the Counter-Thesis would be, "Edmund should have followed the White Witch." After comparing the two theses, you might note (with help from the Essay Five Arrangement student worksheet) that both sides agree that Edmund, did, in fact, follow her. The point of contention, however, is whether he should have.

Unless an essay or discussion clearly articulates where the Division lies (and with it the common ground) it runs the risk of arguing in circles, harming relationships, and failing to resolve real issues.

Elocution : Antithesis
Antithesis is a scheme that arranges contrasting ideas in adjacent clauses that follow the same grammatical pattern. Create Antithesis by asserting a clause, inserting a contrasting conjunction (such as *but*) or (for writers who understand them) a semi-colon, and asserting a second clause that strongly contrasts with the first. Consider the following examples:

- *I'd rather be dirt poor and loved than filthy rich and despised.*

- Woe to you who laugh now, for you will mourn and weep.
- Not that I loved Caesar less, but that I loved Rome more.

To add Antithesis to the essay, identify a sentence or passage that contrasts two or more things (such as Edmund and Peter, Edmund and the White Witch, etc.) and then rewrite the sentence using a parallel structure that emphasizes the contrast. You might want to write, "Peter was a responsible leader but Edmund was an impudent loner," or, "Edmund was cold, hungry and afraid, while the White Witch was warm, fed, and powerful."

Antithesis is a powerful tool for emphasizing the differences between terms and ideas.

ESSAY SIX

Invention: Circumstance
The Topic of Circumstance helps you discover information about your issue by asking what was happening at *the time* of the issue. First, ask what was happening in the situation where the issue arose, then move outward to various locations surrounding the situation.

If you are thinking about whether Edmund should have followed the White Witch, ask what was happening around him when Edmund stumbled upon the White Witch. You can even begin by asking what was happening in Edmund's or the White Witch's mind.

Next, ask what was happening elsewhere in Narnia at the time, or what was happening at the Professor's house, or in London. You are not concerned at this point whether the events are related to the issue; that comes in the next lesson.

Arrangement: A Guide to Refutation
A Refutation is a response to a counter-argument. When you write a Persuasive Essay, you affirm your Thesis by presenting Proofs that support your position. But not everyone will agree, and those who don't will choose the opposing position. In the Refutation, you describe the opposing position and then state why that position is inadequate.

For example, while you might argue that Edmund should not have followed the

White Witch, someone else might argue that he should have. In your Refutation, you list your opponents best reasons (e.g. he was lonely, cold, and hungry) and then you explain why those reasons are insufficient (e.g. they only consider the short term).

To write a Refutation, follow these steps. First, state the Counter-Thesis. This is the statement that opposes your Thesis. Second, choose two of the strongest reasons that support the Counter-Thesis. You have already discovered and sorted the material for these reasons in your ANI, so return to your sorted ANI and select two Proofs from the A or N column. Remember, this will be the position *you did not choose to defend*. Third, list three supports for each Counter-Thesis Proof. Fourth explain why these reasons are not compelling enough. Finally, briefly summarize your Refutation.

Elocution: Simile
A simile is a trope that makes an explicit comparison of two things different in kind but sharing a striking quality. Similes use such comparison words as *like* or *as* to make the comparison explicit.

To write a simile, follow three steps. First, select something in your sentence that you want to emphasize (usually because it has a quality you want to draw out). Second, list some of its characteristics or qualities and select one to highlight. Third, link the first thing to a different kind of thing that shares a similar characteristic or quality by using a comparison word, such as *like* or *as*.

For instance, if you want to emphasize the White Witch, start by listing some of her characteristics and qualities. You might note that she is deceptive. Next, name a different kind of thing that is also deceptive and link the White Witch to that thing with a comparison word. For example, a fisherman deceives to catch a fish. Your simile is, "The White Witch used Turkish Delight to catch Edmund like a fisherman uses bait to catch a fish."

ESSAY SEVEN

Invention: Relation
Using the Topic of Relation, you gather information by listing the events or actions that took place before the situation and those that followed the actor's decision. Next, review the list of preceding actions and events to identify which

might be causes of the situation. Finally, review the list of actions and events that followed the decision to identify which are effects (i.e. are caused by the decision made).

Some essays may look at the Issue assuming that the decision is not yet made. In that case, writers should list possible or probable effects of the affirmative and negative decisions.

For the issue, "Whether Edmund should have followed the White Witch," begin by asking what happened (actions and events) before Edmund met the White Witch. Then ask what happened after Edmund decided to follow the White Witch.

Next, select the actions or events that caused Edmund to be in the situation (confronted by the White Witch in Narnia), and the actions or events caused or probably caused by the decision (effects).

To find actions or events that caused the situation, ask, "What caused the actor to be in this situation?" To find actions or events that the decision caused, ask, "What happened because of the decision made?"

If you assume that Edmund has not yet made his decision, you would ask, "What will likely happen if Edmund does follow the White Witch? What if he doesn't?" This is frequently an excellent perspective to take when students are in the middle of a story or when you are leading a discussion.

Arrangement: A Guide to Narratio
The Narratio is a simple narration of background information that helps the reader understand the context of your thesis. The Narratio is placed before the Thesis in the Template.

The Narratio consists of the situation (time, place, characters), and the events or actions (the causes) that led to the situation. Thus, the Invention lesson on the Topic of Relation prepares students for this lesson.

To write a Narratio, follow these four steps:
- Describe the situation of the issue.

- Generate a list of actions or events that led to the situation by asking, "How did the actor get in this situation? What caused this situation?"

- Ask, "And what caused that cause?"

- Convert this chain of causes into a simple narration.

If you argue that Edmund should not have followed the White Witch, generate a Narratio by asking, "When and where did this take place?" and, "Who was involved?" Edmund is in the White Witch's sleigh during the 100 year Narnian winter.

Then ask, "How did the actor get there?" He walked through a wardrobe. "And what caused that?" He was playing hide and seek with his siblings. "And how did that happen?" They needed something to do while at the Professor's house in the country because of the war.

Elocution: Alliteration
Alliteration is the repetition of initial *consonant* sounds in a phrase or verse. You are perhaps most familiar with the use of alliteration in tongue twisters like, "Peter Piper picked a peck of pickled peppers." Alliteration also gives titles a pleasing rhythm, such as *The Merry Wives of Windsor* or *The Lion, the Witch, and the Wardrobe*. But don't limit the value of alliteration (or assonance, see Essay Nine below) to tongue twisters and titles. Robert Louis Stevenson, one of the finest stylists in the English language, wrote: "The beauty of the contents of a phrase, or of a sentence, depends implicitly upon alliteration and upon assonance. You may follow the adventures of a letter through any passage that has particularly pleased you."

To add alliteration, follow these steps. First, identify a word, phrase, or clause that you want to emphasize or improve with a better sound. Second, identify a consonant sound that you want to repeat. Third, generate a list of words that contain the same consonant sound, and, finally, select several words from the list that fit and add them to your original sentence.

For instance, consider the following sentence, "The White Witch made Narnia a total mess." You might wish to repeat the "w" sounds found in white and witch. You could change the words *total mess* to *wasteland,* and replace the word *made* with *wielded her power*. The new sentence will read, "The White Witch wielded her power and turned Narnia into a wasteland."

ESSAY EIGHT

Invention: Testimony—Witnesses
You will learn to collect testimony (i.e. information) from witnesses. Witnesses can provide two kinds of testimony: direct observation of an action or event within the situation, or an actor's patterns of behavior that extend beyond the situation. Briefly, witness testimony provides firsthand knowledge of an action or of an actor's character.

To collect testimony from witnesses, follow four steps. First, identify witnesses to the situation. Second, list the actions or events they witnessed in the situation. Third, describe patterns of behavior they have witnessed in an actor beyond the situation. Finally, assess the reliability of the witness.
If your issue is, "Whether Edmund should have followed the White Witch," first, identify a witness to the situation, such as the dwarf. Then ask what he saw the White Witch or Edmund do in the situation. He could say that he saw the White Witch make Turkish Delight and put her warm robes around Edmund. Third, ask what patterns he has seen in her behavior. He has seen the White Witch lose her temper on many occasions, turning Narnians into stone. Finally, assess the dwarf's reliability. He is probably not a reliable witness because he is afraid of the White Witch.

You should feel free to use a new witness for the third step if, as is common, the first witness saw the situation, but has not seen the actor in other contexts.

Arrangement: Review
No new content is introduced in this review lesson.

Elocution: Metaphor
A metaphor compares two different kinds of things and draws a striking, implicit comparison. Unlike simile, metaphors avoid using comparison words such as *like or as*, and instead state that one object *is* the other object. In this way, metaphors make an indirect comparison between two things that are different in kind.

To create a metaphor, follow three steps. First, select a thing you want to describe with a metaphor. Second, list one of its characteristics or qualities. Third, think of another thing that shares that quality but is a different kind of thing from the first.

If you want to emphasize the White Witch, you could list some of her characteristics and qualities, like that she is controlling. Next, name a different kind of thing that is also controlling and directly link the White Witch to this object. A puppeteer is controlling, so you might write, "The White Witch is a puppeteer who controls all of Narnia."

ESSAY NINE

Elocution: Assonance

Similar to alliteration, assonance is the repetition of *vowel* sounds in a phrase or verse that emphasizes a key idea or adds a pleasant tone to your sentences. It is generally less obtrusive than alliteration, so it is more artistic and adaptable. To generate assonance, choose words with similar internal vowel sounds and ground them near each other. For example: "Rage, rage against the **dying** of the **light**" (long "i" sound) and, "Wisely and slow, they **stumble** that **run** fast" (short "u" sound).

To add assonance, follow these steps. First, identify a word, phrase, or clause that you want to emphasize or give a better sound. Second, identify a vowel sound that you want to repeat. Third, generate a list of words that contain the same vowel sound, and, finally, select several words from the list that fit and add them to your original sentence.

For instance, to improve the sentence, "Edmund was a selfish brother who betrayed his family for a piece of candy," you could focus on the strong verb "betrayed" and its long *A* sound. By changing *selfish* to *crave* and *piece* to *taste*, you create the following sentence: "Edmund was a power-craving brother who betrayed his family for a taste of candy." The new words make use of the long *A* sound and the sentence sounds at least a little better.

As with all Level One skills, assonance takes time to master. Give your students that time to practice and to use these many tools simply and even badly before you expect them to use them like master artists!

APPENDIX I
SAMPLE ESSAYS

ESSAY ONE

SAMPLE ESSAY A

Edmund should not have followed the White Witch for three reasons: Edmund's sister Lucy warned him that the White Witch was evil, he should have seen that the White Witch was evil, and he acted in secret.

The first reason Edmund should not have followed the White Witch is that his sister Lucy warned him that the White Witch was evil. The second reason Edmund should not have followed the White Witch is that he should have seen that the White Witch was evil. The third reason Edmund should not have followed the White Witch is that he acted in secret.

Edmund should not have followed the White Witch because his sister Lucy warned him that the White Witch was evil, he should have seen that the White Witch was evil, and he acted in secret.

SAMPLE ESSAY A

Della should cut her hair for three reasons: she had something she could sacrifice, for love, and it was Christmas.

The first reason Della should cut her hair is she had something she could sacrifice. The second reason Della should cut her hair is for love. The third reason Della should cut her hair is it was Christmas.

Della should cut her hair because she had something she could sacrifice, for love, and it was Christmas.

ESSAY TWO

SAMPLE ESSAY A

Edmund should not have followed the White Witch for three reasons: Edmund was *reckless, careless, and secretive.*

The first reason Edmund should not have followed the White Witch is that he was reckless. **The White Witch introduced herself to Edmund as "The Queen of Narnia," but Lucy, who had already met with real creatures in Narnia, called her the "White Witch." We know from fairy tales and literature that witches are evil. Therefore, he should not have followed evil.**

The second reason that Edmund should not have followed the White Witch is that he was careless. **Initially, the White Witch was very cruel to Edmund, and his first instinct was to be scared of her. She fed him Turkish Delight only when she wanted to get something from him. Edmund, with his own eyes, should have seen from this interaction that the White Witch was evil.**

The third reason Edmund should not have followed the White Witch is that he was secretive. **In his very core, Edmund knew that he was doing wrong because he secretly left his siblings and the Beavers and did not discuss his plan with them. Instead of acting openly, he snuck away, probably because they would have not gone along with his plan. Edmund knew that he was betraying his family and innocent creatures.**

Edmund should not have followed the White Witch because he was *reckless, careless, and secretive.*

SAMPLE ESSAY B

Della should cut her hair for three reasons: *to sacrifice, to show love, and to celebrate Christmas.*

The first reason Della should cut her hair is *to sacrifice*. Her long hair is the most valuable possession she owns. Della derives great pleasure from catching a glimpse of herself in the small mirror in her flat. To cut her hair will be a permanent decision. Her hair will most likely not grow back to that great length. She may not have much money, but she has a marketable commodity. By giving up her most precious possession, she will change her looks dramatically.

The second reason Della should cut her hair is *to show love*. In the throes of young love, this precious wife desires to show her husband the depth of her love for him. Throughout the story Jim is pictured as a caring provider, tenderly seeing to his wife. It makes perfect sense that Della would want to find a way to return that commitment with a gesture of her own.

The third reason Della should cut her hair is *to celebrate Christmas*. As the season of giving surrounds her, Della is likely reminded everywhere she goes of the approaching holiday. In a large city such as New York, advertisements, shop windows, and newspapers would all serve as reminders that while everyone else may be shopping for his special someone, Della can't. By cutting her hair she can give Jim not only a gift, but also a perfect complement to the family heirloom.

Della should sell her hair to *sacrifice, show love, and celebrate Christmas.*

ESSAY THREE

SAMPLE ESSAY A

What would you do if a pale, white, icy lady asked you to follow her? In *The Lion, The Witch and The Wardrobe*, Edmund had to make this very decision. Edmund should not have followed the White Witch for three reasons: Edmund was reckless, careless, and secretive.

The first reason Edmund should not have followed the White Witch is that he was reckless. The White Witch introduced herself to Edmund as "The Queen of Narnia," but Lucy, who had already met with real creatures in Narnia, called her the "White Witch." We know from fairy tales and literature that witches are evil . Therefore he should not have followed evil.

The second reason that Edmund should not have followed the White Witch is that he was careless. Initially, the White Witch was very cruel to Edmund, and his first instinct was to be scared of her. She fed him Turkish Delight only when she wanted to get something from him. Edmund, with his own eyes, should have seen from this interaction that the White Witch was evil.

The third reason Edmund should not have followed the White Witch is that he was secretive. From his very core, Edmund knew that he was doing wrong because he secretly left his siblings and the Beavers and did not **discuss** his plan with them. Instead of acting openly, he snuck away, probably because they would have not gone along with his plan. Edmund knew that he was betraying his family and innocent creatures.

Edmund should not have followed the White Witch because he was reckless , careless, and secretive.

SAMPLE ESSAY B

Imagine giving up your most precious possession. In the short story "The Gift of the Magi" by O. Henry, the main character was faced with this very challenge. Della should cut her hair for three reasons: to sacrifice, to show love, and to celebrate Christmas.

The first reason Della should cut her hair is *to sacrifice*. Her long hair is the most valuable possession she owns. Della derives great pleasure from catching a glimpse of herself in the small mirror in her flat. To cut her hair off will be a permanent decision. Her hair, most likely, will not grow back to that great length. She may not have much money, but she has a marketable commodity. By giving up her most precious possession, she will change her looks dramatically.

The second reason Della should cut her hair is *to show love*. In the throes of young love, this precious wife desires to show her husband the depth of her love for him. Throughout the story, the author pictures Jim as a caring provider, tenderly seeing to his wife. It makes perfect sense that Della would want to find a way to return that commitment with a gesture of her own.

The third reason Della should cut her hair is *to celebrate Christmas*. As the season of giving surrounds her, festive decorations and fancy shop windows remind Della of the approaching holiday. In a large city such as New York, advertisements, shop windows, and newspapers would all serve as reminders that while everyone else may be shopping for his special someone, Della has no means to do so. By cutting her hair she not only can give Jim a gift, but also a perfect complement to the family heirloom.

Della should sell her hair to *sacrifice, show love, and celebrate Christmas.*

ESSAY FOUR

SAMPLE ESSAY A

What would you do if a pale, white, icy lady asked you to follow her? *In The Lion, The Witch, and The Wardrobe,* Edmund had to make this very decision. Edmund should not have followed the White Witch for three reasons: Edmund **purposely ignored a warning, carelessly overlooked the White Witch, and secretly followed Lucy into Narnia.**

The first reason Edmund should not have followed the White Witch is that he purposely ignored a warning. The White Witch introduced herself to Edmund as "The Queen of Narnia," but Lucy, who had already met with real creatures in Narnia, called her the "White Witch." We know from fairy tales and literature that witches are evil. Therefore he should not have followed evil.

The second reason that Edmund should not have followed the White Witch is that he carelessly overlooked the White Witch. Initially, the White Witch was very cruel to Edmund, and his first instinct was to be scared of her. She fed him Turkish Delight only when she wanted to get something from him. Edmund, with his own eyes, should have seen from this interaction that the White Witch was evil.

The third reason Edmund should not have followed the White Witch was that he secretly followed Lucy into Narnia. From his very core, Edmund knew that he was doing wrong because he secretly left his siblings and the Beavers and did not discuss his plan with them. Instead of acting openly, he snuck away, probably because they would have not gone along with his plan. Edmund knew that he was betraying his family and innocent creatures.

Edmund should not have followed the White Witch because he purposely ignored a warning, carelessly overlooked the White Witch, and secretly followed Lucy into Narnia. **Edmund caused tremendous trouble not only for himself, but—even worse—for his siblings and for all of Narnia.**

SAMPLE ESSAY B

Imagine giving up your most precious possession. In the short story "The Gift of the Magi" by O. Henry, the main character was faced with this very decision. Della should cut her hair for three reasons: **to sacrifice, to show love, and to celebrate Christmas**.

The first reason Della should cut her hair is *to* sacrifice. Her long hair is the most valuable possession she owns. Della derives great pleasure from catching a glimpse of herself in the small mirror in her flat. To cut her hair off will be a permanent decision. Her hair, most likely, will not grow back to that great length. She may not have much money, but she has a marketable commodity. By giving up her most precious possession, she will change her looks dramatically.

The second reason Della should cut her hair is to show love. In the throes of young love, this precious wife desires to show her husband the depth of her love for him. Throughout the story, the author pictures Jim as a caring provider, tenderly seeing to his wife. It makes perfect sense that Della would want to find a way to return that commitment with a gesture of her own.

The third reason Della should cut her hair is to celebrate Christmas. As the season of giving surrounds her, festive decorations and fancy shop windows remind Della of the approaching holiday. In a large city such as New York, advertisements, shop windows, and newspapers would all serve as reminders that while everyone else may be shopping for his special someone, Della has no means to do so. By cutting her hair she not only can give Jim a gift, but also a perfect complement to the family heirloom.

Della should sell her hair to sacrifice, show love, and celebrate Christmas. **This matters to our friends and family, members of our community, as we all need a picture of what Christmas is all about. What matters is not the value of the gifts one receives, but of the gifts one gives.**

ESSAY FIVE

SAMPLE ESSAY A

What would you do if a pale, white, icy lady asked you to follow her? In *The Lion, The Witch, and The Wardrobe,* Edmund had to make this very decision. **Everyone agrees that Edmund followed the White Witch, but some believe that Edmund should have followed her and some believe that he should not have followed her.**

Edmund should not have followed the White Witch for three reasons: Edmund purposely ignored a warning, carelessly overlooked the White Witch, and secretly followed Lucy into Narnia.

The first reason Edmund should not have followed the White Witch is that he purposely ignored a warning. The White Witch introduced herself to Edmund as "The Queen of Narnia," but Lucy, who had already met with real creatures in Narnia, called her the "White Witch." We know from fairy tales and literature that witches are evil. Therefore he should not have followed evil.

The second reason that Edmund should not have followed the White Witch is that he carelessly overlooked the White Witch. Initially, the White Witch was very cruel to Edmund, and his first instinct was to be scared of her. She fed him Turkish Delight only when she wanted to get something from him. Edmund, with his own eyes, should have seen from this interaction that the White Witch was evil.

The third reason Edmund should not have followed the White Witch was that he secretly followed Lucy into Narnia. From his very core, Edmund knew that he was doing wrong because he secretly left his siblings and the Beavers and did not discuss his plan with them. **He could have been honest and open, but he chose to be deceitful and secretive--**probably because they would have not gone along with his plan. Edmund knew that he was betraying his family and innocent creatures.

Edmund should not have followed the White Witch because he purposely ignored a warning, carelessly overlooked the White Witch, and secretly followed Lucy into Narnia. Edmund caused tremendous trouble not only for himself, but—even worse—for his siblings and for all of Narnia.

SAMPLE ESSAY B

Imagine giving up your most precious possession. In the short story, "The Gift of the Magi" by O. Henry, the main character was faced with this very decision. **Everyone agrees that Della greatly desires to give a gift to her husband, Jim, for Christmas; however some feel Della should cut and sell her hair to pay for the gift, while others feel Della should not cut and sell her hair.**

Della should cut her hair for three reasons: to sacrifice, to show love, and to celebrate Christmas.

The first reason Della should cut her hair is to sacrifice. Her long hair is the most valuable possession she owns. Della derives great pleasure from catching a glimpse of herself in the small mirror in her flat.. To cut her hair off will be a permanent decision. Her hair, most likely, will not grow back to that great length. She may not have much money, but she has a marketable commodity. By giving up her most precious possession, she will change her looks dramatically.

The second reason Della should cut her hair is to show love. In the throes of young love, this precious wife desires to show her husband the depth of her love for him. Throughout the story, the author pictures Jim as a caring provider, tenderly seeing to his wife. It makes perfect sense that Della would want to find a way to return that commitment with a gesture of her own.

The third reason Della should cut her hair is to celebrate Christmas. As the season of giving surrounds her, festive decorations and fancy shop windows remind Della of the approaching holiday. In a large city such as New York, advertisements, shop windows, and newspapers would all serve as reminders that while everyone else may be shopping for his special someone, Della has no means to do so. By cutting her hair she not only can give Jim a gift, but also a perfect complement to the family heirloom.

Della should sell her hair to sacrifice, show love, and celebrate Christmas. This matters to our friends and family, members of our community as we all need a picture of what Christmas is all about. What matters is not the value of the gifts one receives, but of the gifts one gives.

ESSAY SIX

SAMPLE ESSAY A

What would you do if a pale, white, icy lady asked you to follow her? In *The Lion, The Witch, and The Wardrobe,* Edmund had to make this very decision. Everyone agrees that Edmund followed the White Witch, but some believe that Edmund should have followed her and some believe that Edmund should not have followed her.

Edmund should not have followed the White Witch for three reasons: Edmund purposely ignored a warning, carelessly overlooked the White Witch, and secretly followed Lucy into Narnia.

The first reason Edmund should not have followed the White Witch is that he purposely ignored a warning. The White Witch introduced herself to Edmund as "The Queen of Narnia," but Lucy, who had already met with real creatures in Narnia, called her the "White Witch." We know from fairy tales and literature that witches are evil. Therefore he should not have followed evil.

The second reason Edmund should not have followed the White Witch is that he carelessly overlooked the White Witch. Initially, the White Witch was very cruel to Edmund, and his first instinct was to be scared of her. She fed him Turkish Delight only when she wanted to get something from him, **like a fisherman feeds a worm on a hook to the fish he wants to catch and eat**. Edmund, with his own eyes, should have seen from this interaction that the White Witch was evil.

The third reason Edmund should not have followed the White Witch is that he secretly followed Lucy into Narnia. From his very core, Edmund knew that he was doing wrong because he secretly left his siblings and the Beavers and did not discuss his plan with them. He could have been honest and open, but he chose to be deceitful and secretive—probably because they would have not gone along with his plan. Edmund knew that he was betraying his family and innocent creatures.

Some people say that Edmund should have followed the White Witch. They argue that the White Witch took care of Edmund, feeding him Turkish Delight and speaking kindly to him. However, this idea is

inadequate because we see the White Witch's true personality later. We see that she did not really care about Edmund, but that she simply wanted to take over Narnia. Feeding Edmund Turkish Delight and speaking kindly to him was just a means to reaching her evil goal.

In addition, people argue that Edmund should have followed the White Witch because he was alone and scared; thus he could not use proper judgment. This argument is also invalid because Edmund was not really alone. He had his trustworthy sister, Lucy, with him, and she had already testified that the White Witch was evil. We know that Edmund followed the White Witch out of pride and selfish ambition.

Neither of these arguments—that the White Witch took care of Edmund, and that Edmund was alone and scared—would give Edmund any sufficient reason to follow the White Witch.

Edmund should not have followed the White Witch because he purposely ignored a warning, carelessly overlooked the White Witch, and secretly followed Lucy into Narnia. Edmund caused tremendous trouble, not only for himself, but—even worse—for his siblings and for all of Narnia.

SAMPLE ESSAY B

Imagine giving up your most precious possession. In the short story "The Gift of the Magi" by O. Henry, the main character was faced with this very decision. Everyone agrees that Della greatly desires to give a gift to her husband, Jim, for Christmas, however some feel Della should cut and sell her hair to pay for the gift while others feel Della should not cut and sell her hair.

Della should cut her hair for three reasons: to sacrifice, to show love, and to celebrate Christmas.

The first reason Della should cut her hair is to sacrifice. Her long hair is the most valuable possession she owns. Della derives great pleasure from catching a glimpse of herself in the small mirror in her flat. ***She feels like a parading peacock***. To cut her hair off will be a permanent decision. Her hair, most likely, will not grow back to that great length. She may not have much money, but she has a marketable commodity. By giving up her most precious possession, she will change her looks dramatically.

The second reason Della should cut her hair is to show love. In the throes of young love, this precious wife desires to show her husband the depth of her love for him. Throughout the story, the author pictures Jim as a caring provider, tenderly seeing to his wife. It makes perfect sense that Della would want to find a way to return that commitment with a gesture of her own.

The third reason Della should cut her hair is to celebrate Christmas. As the season of giving surrounds her, festive decorations and fancy shop windows remind Della of the approaching holiday. In a large city such as New York, advertisements, shop windows, and newspapers would all serve as reminders that while everyone else may be shopping for his special someone, Della has no means to do so. By cutting her hair she not only can give Jim a gift, but also a perfect complement to the family heirloom.

Some claim that Della should not sell her hair. After all, what might her husband's reaction be? Jim might not like her new hairstyle, might not approve of her sacrifice, and might hurt his career by having a wife who looks like a "Coney Island chorus girl." But there is no evidence to support this assertion. Della claims that a new watch chain might in fact help his standing in the community. A husband who would willingly sacrifice his own precious possession surely would not chastise his wife for selling hers.

In addition, some argue that the couple's budget is reason enough to put any spare change into savings. How can they justify such an impractical gift in the face of their present poverty? Jim wears a shabby coat, his salary has recently been reduced, and Della must bargain with the grocers for any savings she can. This reasoning is faulty. Even in the midst of less than ideal circumstances, a grand generous gesture can serve to remind us of the value of true love and sacrifice. Appropriate to the season of giving, Della can give.

Thus, neither Jim's reaction nor the couple's budget is enough to dissuade Della from selling her beautiful, valuable hair.

Della should sell her hair to sacrifice, show love, and celebrate Christmas. This matters to our friends, family, and members of our community as we all need a picture of what Christmas.

ESSAY SEVEN

SAMPLE ESSAY A

What would you do if a pale, white, icy lady asked you to follow her? In *The Lion, The Witch, and The Wardrobe*, Edmund had to make this very decision

One day, while playing hide and seek with his brother and sisters, Edmund followed his younger sister, Lucy, through an old, forgotten wardrobe. Passing through the coats, he found himself in a different world, the world of Narnia. Immediately, Edmund was startled by an icy woman in an icy sleigh. She demanded to know who he was and what he was doing there. After Edmund gorged himself on Turkish Delight, the White Witch insisted that he must visit her at her castle, bringing along his brother and sisters.

Everyone agrees that Edmund followed the White Witch, but some believe that Edmund should have followed her and some believe that Edmund should not have followed her. Edmund should not have followed the White Witch for three reasons: Edmund purposely ignored a warning, carelessly overlooked the White Witch, and secretly followed Lucy into Narnia.

The first reason Edmund should not have followed the White Witch is that he purposely ignored a warning. The White Witch introduced herself to Edmund as "The Queen of Narnia," but Lucy, who had already met with real creatures in Narnia, called her the "White Witch." We know from fairy tales and literature that witches are evil. Therefore he should not have followed evil.

The second reason that Edmund should not have followed the White Witch is that he carelessly overlooked the White Witch. Initially, the White Witch was very cruel to Edmund, and his first instinct was to be scared of her. She fed him Turkish Delight only when she wanted to get something from him, like a fisherman feeds a worm on a hook to the fish he wants to catch and eat. Edmund, with his own eyes, should have seen from this interaction that the White Witch was evil.

The third reason Edmund should not have followed the White Witch is that he secretly followed Lucy into Narnia. From his very core, Edmund knew that he was doing wrong because he secretly left his siblings and the Beavers and did not discuss his plan with them. He could have been honest and open, but he chose to be deceitful and secretive—probably because they would have not gone along with his plan. Edmund knew that he was betraying his family and innocent creatures.

Some people say that Edmund should have followed the White Witch. They argue that the White Witch took care of Edmund, feeding him Turkish Delight and speaking kindly to him. However, this idea is invalid because we see the White Witch's true personality later. We see that she did not really care about Edmund, but that she simply wanted to take over Narnia. Feeding Edmund Turkish Delight and speaking kindly to him was just a means to reaching her evil goal.

In addition, people argue that Edmund should have followed the White Witch because he was alone and scared; thus he could not use proper judgment. This argument is also invalid because Edmund was not really alone. He had his trusted sister, Lucy, with him, and she had already testified that the White Witch was evil. We know that Edmund followed the White Witch out of pride and selfish ambition.

Neither of these arguments—that the White Witch took care of Edmund, and that Edmund was alone and scared—would give Edmund any reason to follow the White Witch.

Edmund should not have followed the White Witch because he purposely ignored a warning, carelessly overlooked the White Witch, and secretly followed Lucy into Narnia. Edmund **caused careless casualties** not only for himself, but—even worse—for his siblings and for all of Narnia.

SAMPLE ESSAY B

Imagine giving up your most precious possession. In the short story "The Gift of the Magi" by O. Henry, the main character was faced with this very decision.

Della and Jim, newlyweds living in New York City, are quickly finding out that married life is not without problems. Jim's salary has been reduced and their financial obligations have remained the same. In spite of her thrift and industry, Della finds herself on Christmas Eve

with less than two dollars with which <u>to purchase a present for her precious</u> husband.

Everyone agrees that Della greatly desires to give a gift to her husband, Jim, for Christmas, however some feel Della should cut and sell her hair to pay for the gift while others feel Della should not cut and sell her hair.

Della should cut her hair for three reasons: to sacrifice, to show love, and to celebrate Christmas.

The first reason Della should cut her hair is to sacrifice. Her long hair is the most valuable possession she owns. Della derives great pleasure from catching a glimpse of herself in the small mirror in her flat. She feels like a queen and *her hair is her crown*. To cut her hair off will be a permanent decision. Her hair, most likely, will not grow back to that great length. She may not have much money, but she has a marketable commodity. By giving up her most precious possession, she will change her looks dramatically.

The second reason Della should cut her hair is to show love. In the throes of young love, this doting wife desires to show her husband the depth of her love for him. Throughout the story, the author pictures Jim as a caring provider, tenderly seeing to his wife. It makes perfect sense that Della would want to find a way to return that commitment with a gesture of her own.

The third reason Della should cut her hair is to celebrate Christmas. As the season of giving surrounds her, festive decorations and fancy shop windows remind Della of the approaching holiday. In a large city such as New York, advertisements, shop windows, and newspapers would all serve as reminders that while everyone else may be shopping for his special someone, Della has no means to do so. By cutting her hair she not only can give Jim a gift, but also a perfect complement to the family heirloom.

Some claim that Della should not sell her hair. After all, what might her husband's reaction be? Jim might not like her new hairstyle, might not approve of her sacrifice, and might hurt his career by having a wife who looks like a "Coney Island chorus girl." But there is no evidence to support this assertion. Della claims that a new watch chain might in fact help his standing in the community. A husband who would willingly sacrifice his own precious possession surely would not chastise his wife for selling hers.

In addition, some argue that the couple's budget is reason enough to put any spare change into savings. How can they justify such an impractical gift in the face of their present poverty? Jim wears a shabby coat, his salary has recently been reduced, and Della must bargain with the grocers for any savings she can. This reasoning is faulty. Even in the midst of less than ideal circumstances, a grand generous gesture can serve to remind us of the value of true love and sacrifice. Appropriate to the season of giving, Della can give.

Thus, neither Jim's potential reaction nor the couple's budget is enough to dissuade Della from selling her beautiful, valuable hair.

Della should sell her hair to sacrifice, show love, and celebrate Christmas. This matters to our friends, family, and members of our community as we all need a picture of what Christmas is all about. What matters is not the value of the gifts one receives, but of the gifts one gives.